Gangster's Guide to God

God bless

John +

I would like to dedicate this book in thanksgiving for the gift of my mum, Joan whose prayers over many years had a profound effect on me meeting God. Her love and support has been truly inspirational. She never gave up on me, I urge all parents to follow her example and not give up on their children.

A Gangster's Guide to God

John Pridmore
With
Greg Watts

St. Patrick's Publishers

First published 2007

Cover design by Dave Moloney

ISBN 978-0-9555714-0-4
A catalogue record for this book is available from the British Library.

Printed by C&R PRINT, Enniscorthy, Co. Wexford, Ireland.
www.crprint.ie

Contents

Acknowledgements

There are many people who have played a part in my life journey; too many to list. So I hope no one will be offended if they are not mentioned. I would like to thank my family, especially my mum and dad (rest in peace), for the love patience and understanding they have shown me throughout my life, through the hard times and the good times. I would like to thank my brother David and his children for the blessings they have been in my life, my brothers Bobby and Simon, sisters Emma and Linda, and both sets of Grandparents.

I must also acknowledge my step-father Alan (rest in peace), who gave me my first copy of the New Testament, and my stepmother Elsie. I would also like to thank Bulldog (rest in peace), Douglas Hewitt, David Pracher (rest in peace), Harry Ward, Gary, Neil Slattery, Robert Toone and all my friends at Youth 2000, Mary Anne and Calum MacFarlane-Barrow at the Family House of Prayer, Dalmally, Scotland, Basilia Abel-Smith, Mary, Lesley, Declan, Dominic, Peter and Richard Jones, Stuart Harris, Alex Beverley, Dougie McVicar and all my Godchildren. I would like to thank Father Brian O'Higgins, whom I first met as a sixteen-year-old when I was in hospital, Father Michael Kelly, who helped me make my first confession and was responsible for me going on my first retreat, Father Pat Deegan, and Father Denis Herlihy, for the wise spiritual direction he has given me.

Many other priests have played an important role in my life. I cannot mention them all, but I would especially like to acknowledge Father Richard Aladics, Father Ian Ker, Father William Fraser, Father Conrad, Father Benedict Groeschel, Father Glen Sudano, Father Richard Romer, Father Bernard Murphy, Father Justin Price and Father Fred de l'Orme, John Roche for his wonderful support and encouragement in Ireland and Father Jim Finn for his continued spiritual guidance.

I must also mention Brother Francis. I must also thank Brendan Walsh without whom the original book would not have seen the light of day, Greg Watts for drawing out my memories, thoughts and reflections over many months.

There is someone else I have to thank, too: Jesus Christ, who is my life and can become yours.

John Pridmore

Chapter 1

The Guv'nor

I always thought that God was a fairy tale, made up to keep people from doing bad things. But that all changed in the summer of 1991, in Central London, after I nearly killed a guy outside a bar owned by a firm I was heavily involved with.

It started when a rowdy group of drinkers in their twenties refused to leave at closing time. This was a common problem when you were working the doors. Myself and several other doormen had managed to get the group out of the bar, but they clearly weren't happy. When one of them tried to push past me to get back in, I slipped on my knuckle-duster and drove my fist into his face. As his head hit the pavement it exploded, splattering blood everywhere. I stood motionless, not knowing what to do. Someone ran into the office to call an ambulance.

'He's dead! He's dead!' screamed a girl.

The next moment, I felt a heavy hand on my shoulder. *'Come on son, you've killed him.'*

It was my mate Bulldog, who had come over from East London to have a drink with me.

'Give me your car keys, John. I'll take your car back and you can get a cab outside Cairos.'

I hurried back into the bar, ran down into the basement, disappeared out the back door, and made my way to Cairos, a club in the next street. Bulldog was waiting there, sitting in my car. I decided not to get a cab, preferring to drive home myself.

'You've killed the bloke, John. You've got to think about what you're going to do,' said Bulldog, as we drove into the West End traffic. He was a top face in the East End and no stranger to this sort of thing.

'Is anyone at the pub going to give the Old Bill your full name?' he asked.

'No. No one will say anything,' I replied, still replaying the incident in my mind.

'Good. Now, do you want some money to go abroad to Spain or somewhere?'

'I've got money, Bulldog,' I answered with a shrug of the shoulders.

'There's no problem. Don't worry. I can handle it.'

Not long after this, I was sitting alone one night in my flat in Leyton, thinking what a mess I'd made of my life. The man I'd hit didn't die. But I'd been arrested and charged with GBH. I was now facing a trial. If I was convicted, I wouldn't get away with a fine; I'd be sent down.

My problems had started when my parents got divorced. That event shattered my world. I quickly lost interest at school and drifted into petty crime. By my late teens, I'd already served time in a detention centre and a youth prison. But they failed to change me.

When I began doing backstage security work at pop concerts, I was introduced to a world of easy money, violence, drugs and women. It wasn't long before I was dealing drugs and then setting up drug deals. The further I got into the underworld the more violent I became. I was 6'4", strong and knew how to handle myself. But I carried a machete and ammonia in my jacket pocket as extra protection. By the age of twenty-seven, I was driving flashy cars, running a luxury penthouse flat, and had more money in my pockets than I knew what to do with.

Something happened as I sat in my flat that night, and it changed my life forever. All of a sudden, I heard what I can only describe as a voice. It told me about all the worst things I'd done in my life. Thinking it must be the TV, I got up and turned it off. But I still heard the voice. I realised it was the voice of my conscience. I felt the breath going out of me, and an incredible fear gripped me. *'I'm going to hell,'* I thought.

I fell to my knees, my eyes filled with tears, and I cried out, *'Give me another chance!'* Suddenly, I felt as if someone's hands were on my shoulders and I was being lifted up. An incredible warmth filled me and the fear disappeared. At that moment I knew – really knew, not just believed – that God was real.

From that point on my life began to change radically. To my relief, the GBH charge I faced was thrown out of court. I began praying, reading the Bible and going to Mass. Although I'd been baptised as a Catholic, it had meant nothing to me up until then.

Fifteen years later, I now want to bring others to an experience of God. I want to show that Christ can transform lives, no matter how broken or messed up, like mine was. The mercy, forgiveness and freedom that I've experienced is available to everyone. All you have to do is ask God into your life and trust in him.

But a lot of people nowadays say they're not sure if they believe in God. It's become almost fashionable. I didn't want God to be real. If God was real, that meant I'd be judged about the things I'd done in my life and end up in hell.

We often want to be God and we feel that we don't need God. Many people live today by their own rules, not the laws of God. It's often pride that blocks our relationship with God. I once had a conversation with an old man who was adamant that God didn't exist. I said, *'Well, why don't you ask God if he's real? You've got nothing to lose.'* But he wouldn't. It was his pride that prevented him from doing this.

Just because you say God isn't real doesn't mean that he disappears in a puff of smoke any more than you would if I said you weren't real. You're real and wandering around the gaff quite happy. And God is real too, and he's also wandering around the gaff quite happy.

I was once asked by a friend to give a talk at Allen Hall seminary in London, where he was training to be a priest. When I asked him what he felt the students needed, he said, *'We need to know about the mystery and wonder of God. We have all the academic stuff, but we're not hearing about the miracles that God is still working today. So share the miracles that God's working in your life.'* I think our world needs to regain a sense of the mystery and wonder of God.

God knows you inside out and he's the one person who accepts you and rejoices in you. His love is unconditional. Whether you hurt a person or comfort them in their distress, God still loves you exactly the same. But if you are hurting someone you put up a barrier to God's love. To be able to really pray from our heart we have to be honest with God and tell him the things that we're sorry for, the things we're pleased with, the things that are good in our life and the things that are bad in our life.

A man once said to Father John Armitage, a priest I know in East London, *'If there's a God, show me that he's real.'* This question threw Father John because he'd never really been asked to show God to someone before. So he put a bucket in front of the man and said, *'Do you believe in mercy?'*

'What do you mean?' asked the man.

'If someone has really hurt you and then comes to tell you how sorry they truly are, would you forgive them?'

'Yes, if he was really sincere and he begged me,' replied the man.

'Do you believe in love?'

'What do you mean by love?'

'Have you got a wife and kids?'

'Yes. And I'd die for them.'

'So you do believe in love?'

'Yes.'

'Do you believe in compassion?'

'What do you mean by compassion?'

'Well, if a man was lying in the road after being hit by a car, would you walk past or help him?'

'Of course I'd help him,' answered the man.

'So you believe in mercy, you believe in love and you believe in compassion. Now, fill that bucket up with mercy, love and compassion.'

'I can't,' replied the man.

'Well,' said Father John, *'I can't show you God either. But you know God exists because you know mercy, love and compassion. That's what God is.'*

I think this story of Father John's cuts through to what God's really about. He's not this headmaster-figure in the sky, watching our every move to see if we slip up so that he can punish us. I'm amazed how many people today have that image of God. God is mercy, love and compassion. And it's in Jesus Christ that we can really see the true image of God. In Jesus, God came to earth to show us what he's really like.

Some people say that they believe in God. I don't believe in God – I know God. And I want to know him more and more. I have no doubts that God is real. I've seen many miracles and situations, which were not coincidences but 'God incidences'.

We live in a world where there are a lot of lies. According to what many polls say, we no longer trust politicians, the media or businesses to tell us the truth. It's through finding Jesus that we really find the truth. The truth of how much God loves me was emphasised in the Mel Gibson film *The Passion of the Christ*. It really brought home to me that, through his crucifixion, Jesus had paid for my sins. This is something the devil tries to keep hidden, because if people know that God loved the world so much that he sent his only Son to us, they'll find the true meaning of life.

If we look around at the marvels of the planet, we can see evidence of God. I'm filled with awe when I watch a TV nature documentary about the incredible variety of animals or sea life. All of this didn't happen by accident. It had a creator behind it. There's no conflict between religion and science here, as some people think. Many scientists nowadays accept that there is a creator. You don't have to take the account of Adam and Eve literally. What the book of Genesis is explaining is not how and when the world was created but that there's a creator who brought it into being.

Mother Teresa once attended a conference of one thousand scientists from all over the world. Holding out a flower in her hand, she said, *'With all the wonder of science you can't create this flower. But God can.'*

I heard a story about an old man who was praying the rosary on a long train journey through France. The man sitting opposite him suddenly said, *'Haven't you heard of the wonder of science?'* He then revealed that he was a scientist and for the next hour the old man listened patiently as he talked all about the wonders of science. *'You see, God doesn't exist,'* he stated matter-of-factly. He then asked the old man if he wanted to hear more.

'Yes', nodded the old man.

'Well give me your card and I'll contact you,' said the scientist.

The old man leaned across and handed him a card – his name was Louis Pasteur, one of the greatest scientists who ever lived.

In the nineteenth century the German philosopher Friedrich Nietzsche famously claimed, *'God is dead.'* After his death, someone in New York sprayed on a subway train, *'Nietzsche is dead – God'*.

Father Benedict Groeschel, who founded the Franciscan Friars of the Renewal in New York, says, *'People who believe in science without God are stupid.'* When someone once said to Padre Pio, *'I don't believe in God,'* he replied, *'That's because you're a fool.'*

When I was in prison in my teens I read a book about Robert Ellis, a New York policeman serving a prison sentence for double murder. One day, a minister came up to him on the wing.

'Jesus loves you,' he said.

'Get out of my sight,' snapped back Ellis.

The minister ignored him and continued, *'Ask God if he's real and if he loves you. Is there nothing you want from God?'*

'No, nothing,' growled Ellis.

Ellis had a son, but had never seen him. He'd been born after his trial, and soon after, his wife had divorced him. But after the minister had gone he knelt down in his cell and he prayed, *'Okay, God, if you're real let me see my son.'*

The next day, a prison officer told him he had a visitor. Ellis was surprised, as he never received any visitors. He went with the officer to the visiting room and, to his amazement, sitting there were his ex-wife and his eight-year-old son.

'What has made you come to see me?' he asked, with tears in his eyes.

'I don't know,' said his ex-wife, shaking her head. *'Something told me to come.'*

After this, Ellis was so overcome that he invited God into his life. Something told him that what had happened could only be because God had answered his prayer.

****
****

Something to think about

Yahweh, you examine me and know
me,
you know when I sit, when I rise,
you understand my thoughts from
afar.
You watch when I walk or lie down,
you know every detail of my conduct.

Psalm 139

Chapter 2

Bowled over

I remember the time I worked at a club in London's West End and two guys began hassling me on the door because their names weren't on the guest list. When I politely explained that I couldn't let them in, they wouldn't have it and kept arguing with me.

'You think you're hard, but you're not,' taunted the first one.

'Yeah?' I could feel my anger rising.

'Yeah. You're not hard,' laughed the other guy.

Quickly reaching behind the door, I grabbed a baseball bat and whacked one of them across the head, splitting it open, and then laid into both of them with my fists. I was unstoppable.

Yet I knew they were no real threat to me. I just wanted to impress the girl who was in charge of the guest list. I was going out with her.

In the underworld it was violence that counted, not love. You always had to be harder and more violent than the people around you. Any sign of compassion and mercy was seen as a sign of weakness.

During my year with the Franciscan Friars of the Renewal in the South Bronx, I met Mother Teresa when she came to visit the house she'd established to serve the poor there. Her young, mainly Indian, sisters had tremendous respect on the streets of New York because their lives were dedicated to helping down-and-outs, drug addicts, alcoholics and others who were washed up.

I can recall looking at Mother Teresa as she knelt in the small chapel and thinking how incredibly serene she looked and how she radiated God's love. She had surrendered herself entirely to God's will and was able to see Christ in the faces of the poor.

Through the incarnation God knows what it's like to be human. Jesus became one of us. Father Roddy McCally once told me about a tramp called Jim who would go into his church in Glasgow every day at 3 p.m. and pray for ten minutes. Curious, Father Roddy eventually went up to him and asked why he came into the church at the same time every day.

'I do this because I know that Jesus

died for me at 3 p.m.,' said the tramp. *'I kneel down, say "Hi, Jesus, it's Jim", and I just tell him what's going on with my life.'*

These visits went on for a number of years, and Father Roddy would often invite Jim in for a cup of tea and a sandwich. Then suddenly Jim stopped going to the church. Naturally, Father Roddy wondered what had happened to him.

One afternoon, he was visiting Glasgow Central Hospital when a doctor told him that people were being miraculously healed on one of the wards because of an old man who had been admitted. When Father Roddy walked into the ward, he nearly fell over at the overpowering presence of God. Then he saw Jim lying there.

'Jim,' he said, *'this is amazing. People are being healed and there's such a feeling of God here.'* Jim looked up at him from his bed and said, *'It's nothing to do with me, Father. Every day at 3 p.m. a man stands at the end of my bed and says, "Hi, Jim. It's Jesus."'*

I once went to a category A prison on the Isle of Sheppey to give a talk. Around eighty guys turned up. One of the prison officers told me that sixty per cent of them were in for life and the rest in for ten years or more. *'Many of them are in for murder,'* he added grimly.

Walking into the chapel, I saw about forty guys sitting there, their faces impassive. With their bulging biceps, tattoos and shaved heads, I got a strong sense of the macho world in which they lived.

When I reached the front of the chapel, I knelt down in front of the statue of Our Lady and I prayed silently, *'What is it that your children need?'* I felt her say to me, *'they need hope.'*

I began my talk by telling them how I'd been exactly where they were. I'd been very violent and just concerned about my reputation. And I'd reached a point where I almost had no conscience. *'But I found something that was far more powerful,'* I said. *'I found the grace of love, and it destroyed violence and anger. It's sometimes said that real men don't cry. But I cried when I met Jesus personally.'*

By the time I'd finished the talk, many of these hard men were wiping tears from their eyes. I knew that they felt there was hope and a reason to live. They saw that there was a God and, despite what they may have done, they could be forgiven. Many people looked at these men as the lowest of the low. But the reality was that they were wounded and broken children.

On another occasion, I went along with Father Marius, a religious brother, and a young Missionary of Charity sister to Spofford Youth prison in The Bronx, New York. It was an awful place. The kids were aged between twelve and seventeen and most had been convicted of murder or rape.

'How many of you believe God loves you?' asked the sister, beginning her talk. *'Put your hands up.'*

Not one kid put up his hand. They all just sat there with blank expressions on their faces.

'How many of you believe that the Devil is real?' asked the sister.

I watched as every hand went up.

'You believe that God can't love you because you think you are evil,' she said. *'But that's a lie. And it's the Devil who is telling you this. The truth is that God loves you and accepts you, despite what you have done. All he wants you to do is to tell him that you are sorry. But the Devil tells you that you are no good and that you can't be forgiven.'*

On the way out of the prison, the brother turned to Father Marius and said, *'I also really needed to hear what the sister said.'*

Father Marius nodded and said, *'So did I.'*

Father Marius went to Spofford some time later and one of the Missionaries of Charity came up to him and said, *'Father, I think these boys need confession.'*

'These boys? You must be joking. They never go to confession.'

But Father Marius told the boys that he was available for confession if anyone wanted to go. He sat in the corner of the chapel and waited, but none of the boys left their seats.

'Father, I think the boys need encouragement,' suggested the sister.

Father Marius stood up and said to the boys, *'If any of you are man enough to tell Jesus what you are sorry for, I'm waiting over there.'*

He sat there for five minutes and then one of the boys slowly approached him. It was known that he'd committed a double murder. He began his confession but refused to look Father Marius in the eye. *'Look at me,'* said Father Marius, gently.

The boy looked up.

'Jesus loves you,' said Father Marius.

As soon as he said this, the boy's head dropped and he began to sob.

During that afternoon, ten boys came to him for confession, and when he told each of them that Jesus loved them they too broke down.

The truth is that none of us is worthy of the love of God, but God still loves us. He loves us because of who he is not because of what we have done.

A boy in Germany once e-mailed me to say that his mum had died and he felt he was in darkness and that he wanted the light I seemed to have in my life. *'How do I find this light?'* he asked. I e-mailed him back and urged him to ask Jesus to reveal himself and then to read John's gospel. A few weeks later, I received another e-mail from him. *'John, I can now feel the light coming into my life. And I know that my mum is with Jesus.'*

As we open ourselves up to God and allow his grace to work in our lives, we begin to change. But change doesn't happen overnight. When I first found God, I still carried on smoking dope, being aggressive, and sleeping around. Slowly, he changed my life. But I still have my struggles, even today. Apart from Christianity, all the world's faiths say that you have to obtain perfection to reach God. The Christian message is that God loves us so much that he came to be one of us and that he will bring us to him.

Pope Benedict XVI says of the incarnation, *'God is so great that he can become small. God is so powerful that he can make himself vulnerable and come to us as a defenceless child, so that we can love him.'*

In his book, *A Father Who Keeps His Promises*, Scott Hahn says:

'Let's face it, we humans really don't want God to love us that much. It's simply too demanding. Obedience is one thing, but this sort of love clearly calls for more than keeping commandments. It calls for nothing less than total self-donation. That might not be a difficult job for the infinite Persons of the Trinity, but for creatures like us, such love is a summons to martyrdom. This invitation requires much more suffering and self-denial than simply giving up chocolate for Lent. It demands nothing less than a constant dying to self.'

****
****

Something to think about

For this is how God loved the world:
he gave his only Son,
so that everyone who believes in him
may not perish
but may have eternal life.

John 3:16

Chapter 3

Diamond Geezer

I'll never forget the time the father of a man I'd just beaten up came up to me in a pub where I was drinking and started ranting at me. He might have been in his sixties, but I wasn't going to allow him to talk to me in this way in front of other drinkers. Swiping a glass off the table, I slammed it into his face. It shattered immediately and he collapsed in agony on to the floor.

After I found God, memories of violent incidents such as this haunted me. How could God forgive me? I went to a retreat at Aylesford Priory in Kent and the first talk I heard was called *Give Me Your Wounded Heart*. I listened to a priest explain how every sin we commit is like a wound in our heart. Looking at the crucifix, I realised for the first time in my life why Jesus had died on the cross. The darkest, most sinful things I committed, he gladly carried in his heart to that crucifixion.

I was filled with real sorrow for my sins. But more than this I felt an incredible joy. I felt Jesus say to me, *'John, I love you so much that I would die over and over again for you.'* I felt overwhelmed by this ultimate love and sacrifice, at how an innocent man had died for me personally, so that my sins could be forgiven.

A friend of mine once worked with some poor mountain people in America. One day, one of the men asked him if he would build a porch onto a house. He thought this was a strange request, as the house had no electricity or running water, but he did as he was asked. He spent two weeks building the porch and during that time he realised that he'd never met anyone who was so happy. When he'd finished the porch, he asked the man what his secret was.

'It's because I know Jesus,' said the man.

'But I know Jesus, too,' replied my friend. *'I go to Mass and I pray.'*

'No, you don't know Jesus,' said the man. *'You might know him in your head, but you don't know him in your heart.'*

That night, my friend went home and said to Jesus, *'I don't want to know you in my head anymore. I want to know you personally, in my heart.'* He experienced such love that he spent most of the night crying. In the morning he knew that he was going to give the rest of his life to Jesus. That young man was Father Bernard Murphy, who is now a member of the Franciscan Friars of the Renewal in New York.

Malcolm Muggeridge once wrote, *'Jesus, for me, has been a long process of discovery – a process that is by no means over, and never can be. Like an infinitely precious and rewarding human relationship which goes on developing and constantly reveals new depths and possibilities of intimacy.'*

Father Benedict Groeschel tells a story about the time he went to celebrate Easter at dawn in the open air as the sun rose. He heard someone in the crowd say the word *'shalom'*. Turning around, he saw a rabbi friend of his standing there.

'What are you doing here?' he asked, surprised.

'Oh, I wanted to see what you Christians got up to.'

When a Presbyterian minister began to preach, he said that if Christ didn't rise from the dead, then it didn't really matter.

The rabbi was a bit puzzled and whispered to Father Benedict, *'Well, if Christ didn't rise from the dead, then what are you all doing here?'*

If Christ didn't rise from the dead, then why did the Apostles change so dramatically? Before the crucifixion they were a bumbling group of idiots, and they ran away when he was arrested. To me it seems logical that if you see someone who is resurrected then you wouldn't have any fear of death any more. Look at Peter. When challenged by a servant girl, following the arrest of Jesus, he denied that he knew Jesus. Yet, years later in Rome, he was crucified for his faith in Christ. He asked to be crucified upside down because he didn't feel worthy to be crucified in the way that Jesus had been.

If you read *The Acts of the Apostles* – which is a great adventure story – you have to ask: what was it that gave those Apostles such conviction and drove them to risk their lives by preaching Christ all over the Mediterranean world? The answer is their belief that Christ rose from the dead and that the Holy Spirit was with them.

The fact that many people today don't accept that Jesus Christ was God doesn't make this any less true. In the same way, if the majority of people say something is true it doesn't mean it is. In other words, truth isn't a democracy. In the world today the truths proclaimed by Christ and his Church are often ridiculed. The media frequently makes Christianity out to be archaic and irrelevant and promotes lies and deception about it.

As Malcolm Muggeridge said, *'The Cross is where history and life, legend and reality, time and eternity, intersect. There, Jesus is nailed for ever to show us how God could become man and man could become God.'*

We know from historians of the first century that there was a man called Jesus Christ. This is an indisputable fact. Jesus isn't a character from a fairy tale. Recent archaeological digs in the Holy Land back up the details of the gospels. The four gospels give us different insights into his life, but they all show that he was no ordinary man. It's only in Jesus that we can see what God is really like. The prophets of the Old Testament only gained a glimpse of God. As John's gospel says:

'In the beginning was the Word:
the Word was with God
and the Word was God.
He was with God in the beginning.
Through him all things came to be,
not one thing had its being but through him.'

John is saying that Jesus was not just a prophet or holy man; he was God.

In his letter to the Phillipians, St Paul wrote of Jesus:

'But he emptied himself,
taking the form of a slave,
becoming as human beings are.'

If we're standing on one side of a big void and God is on the other, how do you get across? It's Christ's crucifixion that's our bridge to heaven. Jesus didn't die to avenge an angry God. He died to reconcile us with God. He freely gave his life for us.

As that man who lived in the mountains said, *'the journey to God has to start in the heart, not the head.'* When I give talks in schools and parishes or at retreats, I share my heart with people.

After a retreat in Plymouth one time, a priest said to me, *'I know why you have such a massive effect on kids.'*

'*Why?*' I asked.

'You make yourself vulnerable just like Jesus made himself vulnerable. And the kids feel they have to embrace this vulnerability.'

One time, I was at Mass in Walthamstow on the Feast of the Transfiguration, which recalls when Jesus was transformed on the mountain. Sitting there at the back of the church, looking at the tabernacle, I felt how awesome it was that this piece of bread was actually the creator of the universe. And I felt how incredible it was that God knew me intimately and was my best friend, despite all the billions of people in the world.

It's a bit like going into an art gallery and seeing paintings of Jesus as God on one side of the wall and paintings of Jesus as a man on the other side. You have to put both pictures together to see the real Jesus, divine and human. If you only have one picture you only see a partial image of him.

At Jesus' crucifixion, a Roman centurion declared, *'In truth this man was the Son of God.'* If we open our hearts to Jesus, we will find that he is our total fulfilment on our road to heaven.

****
****

Something to think about

In prayer, united with Jesus – your brother, your friend, your saviour, your God – you begin to breathe a new atmosphere. You form new goals and new ideals. Yes, in Christ you begin to understand yourselves more fully.

Pope John Paul II

Chapter 4

In The Dock

I didn't know the meaning of mercy when I was a gangster. One time, I got into a fight with a man in a pub and ended up getting stabbed. Afterwards, I was seething with anger and I decided to hunt him down and extract my revenge.

It took me a while to find him. Then one afternoon, I spotted him coming out of the school gates with his son. An uncontrollable rage welled up inside of me as I stormed across the road towards him. When he saw me and the look on my face, he was petrified. I beat him senseless, ignoring his plea for mercy and also the screams of frightened parents and children. Yet, as I walked away I didn't feel elated; I felt utterly empty.

It was when I went to confession for the first time in my life that I truly experienced what mercy was. As I told the priest in Westminster Cathedral the worst things I'd ever done, I felt peace and forgiveness flow through me. Afterwards, kneeling in the Lady Chapel, I slowly prayed the Our Father. As I did, it really hit me that God was my father, and I felt like the prodigal son returning to him.

I now understand that revenge is not the answer, no matter how angry you feel. The only answer when someone wrongs you is to show forgiveness and mercy. Through prayer and imitating Christ, I no longer see violence as a solution to a problem. That's not to say I don't get angry from time to time. If someone cuts me up when I'm driving, I can feel anger. And my brothers and sisters in the community I live in will tell you that there are times when I'll blow my top. The difference is that now I realise what's happening and don't let the situation spiral out of control. And I apologise.

Think how Jesus must have felt during his passion. He was betrayed, abandoned, insulted, humiliated and given a brutal whipping by Roman soldiers. He was nailed to a cross and left to face an agonising death. If you've seen Mel Gibson's film *The Passion of the Christ*, you'll have some idea of the pain and suffering that he went through. Yet, despite all of this, he refused to react through violence. He could have called on angels to defend him, but he didn't.

There were many people in my life

who I had to learn to forgive: my parents for getting divorced and those who abused or rejected me. When I was praying about this, I asked God why I had to forgive them all. I heard God say that I, too, had hurt people and they had to forgive me. When we forgive, we are forgiven and when we don't forgive we're not forgiven. A friend of mine who had been abused as a child used to hold a lot of hatred against the man who had done it. When she found Jesus she still found it very hard to forgive him. But she then came to see that all the hatred she felt for this man hadn't affected him one bit – but it had affected her. It had caused her pain, anger, self hatred, and led to her taking drugs and becoming promiscuous.

I heard the story of a former head of the Ulster Defence Force (UDF) who was sent to the Maze prison for trying to blow up a Catholic pub. While he was there he became a Christian.

However, his wife split up with him, and she and their five-year-old son moved in with another man. The relationship became stormy and one night the boyfriend flew into a rage and threw the boy against the wall, smashing his head. The force was so great that he suffered brain damage. The boyfriend was sent to prison – the Maze.

Even though the former UDF man was a Christian, he ran part of the prison. When he heard that the man who was responsible for his son's brain damage was coming to the prison, he resolved to kill him. On the day he planned to exact his revenge he heard God say to him, '*Forgive him.*'

'*But I think you're forgetting what he did to my son,*' said the man.

'*And I think you're forgetting what you did to my son,*' replied God.

The next day, he walked into the man's cell, holding a knife. Seeing him standing there, the other man froze in fear, thinking he was going to be stabbed to death. But the UDF man put the knife on the table and placed his arms around him and said gently, '*I forgive you.*' As he walked back out of that cell, he knew he was now truly a Christian.

At the Edinburgh Festival in 2005 I took part in a TV debate about violence in society with a self-confessed Glasgow gangster, Paul Ferris, TV documentary maker Donald McIntyre and Ann Widdecombe MP. Miss Widdecombe was asked why she thought people on a London bus a few weeks before had ignored a man who had been stabbed for no reason and left for dead. She said that she remembered the days in Britain when people went to church and put God first. If people don't believe in God, she went on, then they have no reason to show mercy. She was right. A world without grace is a world that falls apart.

St John of the Cross once said, '*The weakness we condemn today in another, is the sin into which we will fall ourselves tomorrow, unless God's grace preserves us.*'

The film *The Fisher King* is a great example of grace and forgiveness. Jeff Bridges plays a loud-mouth talk show host who sinks into deep depression after his on-air comments prompt a caller to gun down diners in a restaurant. One day he meets a homeless man, played by Robin Williams. He learns that he was once a professor and is on a mission to find the Holy Grail. When he discovers that his wife was one of those murdered in the restaurant, he is overcome by guilt and offers him money. The homeless man refuses and asks him to accompany him on his search for the Grail. He reluctantly agrees. Their search leads to the talk show host finding forgiveness and redemption.

During World War Two, some SS officers arrived at a hotel in Germany run by a Jewish couple who had both become Christians. As they were booking in, the husband enquired where they had come from.

'*We've just exterminated some Jews at a village near the border,*' replied one of them, laughing.

'*Which one?*' asked the husband.

When the officer told him the name of the village, he went quiet for a moment and then asked, '*Do you believe in mercy and forgiveness?*'

The officer looked puzzled. '*I've been killing people for the last two years. I've probably killed a thousand a day. What do you mean do I believe in mercy and forgiveness?*'

'My wife will show you what it is to forgive,' said the owner.

He then called upstairs to his wife. When she came down, he pointed to the officer and said, *'This man has just returned from your home village. He killed your mother, your father, your grandparents and your brothers and sisters.'*

Hearing this, she threw herself violently onto the floor and then, getting up, walked slowly over to the SS officer and kissed him on the cheek and murmured, *'Through the death of Jesus Christ I forgive you in his name.'*

The SS officer looked stunned. He was so affected by this incident that he later invited Jesus into his life.

I'll never forget meeting a man who was alleged to have killed twenty-five people, even though he had only been convicted of two murders. He was a notorious gangster who had scalped people, cut their hands off, done really horrific things. He tried to justify what he had done by the hurt he had suffered in his childhood. He said that the evil he carried out was nothing compared to what he'd experienced as a kid. I felt he was sick. What he did was unjustifiable. Yet I knew that what he was really crying out for was to be redeemed.

Pope John Paul II gave the world a lesson in forgiveness in 1983 when he visited Mehmet Ali Agca in prison. Agca had tried to assassinate him in St Peter's Square in 1981. Bishop John Magee, Pope John Paul's secretary at the time, told me that when Pope John Paul walked into Agca's cell, he had to be physically held back from embracing him. Bishop Magee said it reminded him of the father embracing the prodigal son. When Agca asked the pope to forgive him, he did so without hesitation. Six months later, Agca asked to become a Catholic. He was reported as saying, *'Wherever there is such mercy God must surely be.'*

Forgiveness is hard, but if you don't forgive, the only person who suffers is you. We don't necessarily forget when we forgive, but we let go of something that has a negative effect in our life. If God forgives us, then why shouldn't we forgive others? In his famous prayer, St Francis of Assisi said, *'For it is in forgiving that we are forgiven.'*

When we fail to see someone as Christ and end up hurting them, we need to go to confession. I often think of confession as a bit like a trial. The Father is the judge, the Devil is the prosecutor, the Holy Spirit is our advocate or defence. The Devil says, *'Look what he's done. He deserves to die.'* When the Spirit calls his first witness, it's Jesus dying on the cross. The Father immediately says, *'Case dismissed.'*

At a retreat at a school in Dublin one time, a young woman came up to me and admitted that she'd been taking drugs and sleeping around.

'I didn't really want to come here, but a friend persuaded me. I'm so glad that I did though,' she said.

'Why?' I asked, feeling that I knew the answer already.

'Because I've been to confession for the first time in years and I now feel that I have God in my life. I only took the drugs and slept around because I hated myself. I was very unhappy.'

I said to her, *'Every time you look in the mirror I want you to say to yourself that you are beautiful and loved by God.'*

One of my favourite films is *Ben Hur*, starring Charlton Heston. Set in the Roman Empire of the first century, it's about the fortunes of two friends, Ben Hur, a Jewish aristocrat and Messala, a Roman army officer. But the film's also about Christ. We see him in the early part of the film, giving a drink to Ben Hur, who has become a Roman slave, and we see him towards the end of the film, struggling through the streets of Jerusalem, carrying his cross.

Ben Hur is a great film about the mercy of God. When I watched it as a kid I just saw the chariot races and all the stuff about the Roman Empire. But when I watched it after I found God, I cried nearly all the way through it. It's a beautiful story of God's love for us and also of forgiveness. Ben Hur learns to forgive his best friend for condemning him to slavery and sending his mother and sister to prison.

I often think our heart is like a window. On one side is God's love, pouring down every minute of the day and on the other side is the stain of our sin. Eventually, we can't see how much we are loved. When we go to confession we take all our sin with us and we come back to life again through God's great love and mercy. I believe God's greatest attribute is his mercy. He's a God who loves to forgive. When we confess our sins we receive that mercy and love.

When I was seven years old, I got a rose bush thorn embedded in my hand. I was petrified that my mum would get a needle and dig it out, so I hid it from her for three days. For the first two days it was incredibly painful, but by the third day it was only if I banged my hand that I was reminded of the thorn. But my mum saw it and she immediately took it out. I thought to myself, 'why didn't I tell my mum about the thorn straightaway?'

When Jesus looks at you he sees every pain and hurt in your life and he sees your sins as thorns piercing your heart. And he wants to take them out. But the only way he can do this is by you giving them to him. He's not just content to take them away. He wants to caress the very place where that sin was. If I had left that thorn in my hand, it would have become infected. In the same way, if I leave my sins in my heart that will infect me in a spiritual way. But if I give my sins to Jesus in confession he will take away my pain.

Someone said to me that when we die we'll have to watch a video of our life. And watching it with us will be Jesus, Mary and all our family and friends.

I said, *'I don't want to watch a video of some of the things I've done in my life.'*

He replied, *'Whatever we brought to confession won't be there. In its place will be a man dying on a cross, saying, "Forgive them, Father, for they know not what they do."'* Newspapers often describe murderers such as Myra Hindley and Ian Huntley as monsters. But we should never make anyone out to be a monster. What someone like this has done might be monstrous, but they are not monsters. When I was a vicious gangster I don't know how many kids I hurt through the drugs and the other stuff I was involved in. But God's mercy is there, even for someone like me. And I know how much pain and guilt I had to go through because of the sins of my past.

Sister Briege McKenna once came to a parish in Ireland to give a talk, and she asked the parish priest if he knew where she'd just come from.

'*No. Where?*' he answered.

She then told him she'd been to see a priest who had been sentenced to seven years in prison for abusing children. Then she added, '*None of you priests have been to see him in the two years he's been in prison, yet you call yourselves Christians. And do you know what he's doing every day?*'

The parish priest shook his head.

'*He's praying and saying Mass for those children he abused. He's repented of his sins.*'

The next day, the parish priest went to visit the priest in prison.

With any sin, no matter how terrible, I always think of Jesus' words: '*Let him who is without sin cast the first stone.*'

When I was helping to run a retreat in Dublin one time, I noticed that all the kids went to confession except one girl. I prayed that she might have the courage to do this. '*Jesus, if I can say anything that might help her, then let it happen.*' That evening, I went out with a friend to a Chinese restaurant for a meal. When I returned to the retreat centre, I went into the church to spend some time in adoration, which was going throughout the night. After a while, I went into the centre for a cup of coffee. I saw the girl there, sitting with two friends.

'*Can I have a word with you?*' I asked.

She looked startled for a moment. '*Yes,*' she said, getting up and following me outside.

'*I know the reason you didn't go to confession,*' I said.

'*No you don't. No one knows me. My boyfriend doesn't know me, nor does my Dad or my Mum. None of them know me,*' she replied curtly.

'*You're wrong. God knows you. And I can prove it. You didn't go to confession because you were sexually abused when you were younger,*' I found myself saying.

She looked shocked when I said this and then burst into tears. After a while she said, '*How did you know?*'

'*I didn't know. Jesus told me. I under-*

stand how you feel. The reason you wouldn't go to confession is because you were scared because you thought you had to confess what happened to you. But you don't have to confess it because you've done nothing wrong. You're innocent. It's the person who did this to you who should confess. If you feel a lot of anger against the person who has hurt you, confess that.'

She then went on to tell me how a family friend had abused her when she was ten years old. That night, I prayed that she would go to confession the following day. She did and afterwards she came running down the corridor to where I was talking to someone and threw her arms around me.

'You were right, God does know me,' she said excitedly, *'and I've just met him!'*

It's in our weaknesses that God uses us. God never asks us to be perfect or good but to try. It doesn't matter how many times we fall. What's important is that we get up each time when we do.

****
****

Something to think about

While he was still a long way off, his father saw him and was moved with pity. He ran to the boy, clasped him in his arms and kissed him. Then his son said, *'Father, I have sinned against heaven and against you. I no longer deserve to be called your son.'* But the father said to his servants, *'Quick! Bring out the best robe and put it on him; put a ring on his finger and sandals on his feet. Bring the calf we have been fattening, and kill it; we will celebrate by having a feast, because this son of mine was dead and has come back to life; he was lost and is found.'* And they began to celebrate.

Luke 15: 20–24

Chapter 5

Get Over It

After I nearly killed that man outside that West End pub in 1991 I started to feel what I now know to be the burden of the sins I was carrying. The faces of many of the people I'd hurt and the girls I'd slept with began to flash through my mind. All the bad things I'd done kept on cropping up. I saw myself as I really was, without the camouflage of power, reputation and money. It was as if someone had held up a mirror to me – but it was a mirror that showed the inside, not the outside

Following that experience of God in my flat, I knew that God had forgiven me for the sins I had committed, but I found it difficult to forgive myself. I would sometimes walk six or seven miles through the streets barefoot and I'd fast for a week, eating nothing and drinking only water. I often slept on the floor. I offered up these penances for the people I'd hurt in the past.

Many of us find it hard to forgive ourselves. A year or so after my conversion I was going through a very difficult time because I still couldn't forgive myself for some of the things I had done. A stranger came up to me one day and said, *'You think you're God.'*

Taken aback, I replied, *'No, I don't.'*

'Yes you do,' he said.

'No, I don't,' I repeated.

'Well, why do you presume to judge yourself,' he said. *'God is the judge and he is far more merciful than you.'*

When he said this, I realised that the reason I couldn't forgive myself was because of pride. I couldn't humble myself. I was judging myself rather than allowing God to judge me.

After giving a talk once about how God loves us and accepts us in our sexuality, a nineteen-year-old guy came up to me. I could see there was something on his mind, so I asked him if he wanted to chat.

'I don't think I have the courage,' he replied.

'Let me say a prayer with you,' I said, *'and afterwards we can have a chat if you want to.'*

He went away and returned half an hour later and told me that he wanted to talk. He went on to say that he'd been sexually abused as a child and had then started having gay sex at the age of fifteen. As he told me about his life, I could see that there was a real self-hatred in him, and that he couldn't believe God could love him. I started to explain that God did love him and he saw all his promiscuous behaviour as part of his wounds from childhood.

I prayed with him and saw a picture of Jesus crying and saying, *'I never wanted you to suffer. I never wanted you to be hurt like this.'* A picture of Our Lady came to me, and she was calling the young guy to her. I told him that she was calling him back to Jesus but he hadn't realised it, and that she was so happy because he was coming back to her son. I felt I could see his heart as Jesus saw it. I didn't see the sin, all I saw was this beautiful soul who God loved.

'When I was a child I used to have a deep devotion to Mary,' he said through the tears. *'I used to pray the rosary each day. But I stopped when I started to sleep around with this older man I met. He used to give me alcohol and cigarettes if I had sex with him. I felt too guilty to pray.'*

I told him the story of the man who used to go to a well each morning, fill up two buckets with water and then walk back to his master's house.

One day, one of the buckets says, *'Throw me away. I have a hole in me. I can only bring half the water the other bucket can.'*

The man replies that the bucket is still useful, even though it has a hole in it. *'No, throw me away,'* repeats the bucket. The man then takes the bucket along the path. *'Look,'* he says, *'on your side of the path there are all these beautiful flowers, but on the other side, where no water has leaked, there are none. Where you leak, you water the master's garden and bring life and joy. The other bucket is perfect, but it doesn't bring any life or joy to the garden.'* If we were perfect, we wouldn't need redemption and forgiveness. Jesus told the story about the Pharisee and the tax collector praying in the Temple. The Pharisee thanked God that he was not grasping, adulterous and unjust. He added that he fasted twice a week and paid his tithes. But the tax collector, standing some distance away, prayed simply, *'God, be merciful to me, a sinner.'*

Sometimes we can take our eyes from what God's calling us to do and become preoccupied with our struggles and our sins and selfishness. Archbishop Fulton Sheen once said that if you look at your weaknesses and darkness, the black hole of original sin will swallow you up. I have to keep on giving my struggles to God. When we fall, whether it's through greed, lust or pride, whatever it is, we need to ask God for healing. But we shouldn't beat ourselves up. A friend of mine who developed a brain tumour when he was in his thirties once said to me, '*Why is it that when I fall down I don't get straight back up and say sorry to Jesus? Why do I spend a month hitting myself over the head with a big club that the Devil gives me?*

God's mercy is always there if we ask for it, but we tend to limit it. If we've sinned four times in a day, for example, we think God can't forgive us. We place conditions on his love. We think to ourselves, well, you might have forgiven me the first time, and maybe the second, but you won't forgive me the third or fourth time. Yet God's love and mercy are limitless. When Peter asked Jesus how many times he should forgive someone who had wronged him, Jesus replied, '*I don't say seven times, but seventy-seven times.*' We must be like God and never stop forgiving.

God will never refuse even the worst sinner in the world, if you say you're sorry. St Therese of Lisieux once said that if she woke up one morning and found she'd committed all the sins it was possible to commit, they would all be as a single drip of water falling into the mouth of a live volcano, which would be God's mercy.

No matter what we may have done, or not done, we're never cut off from the mercy of God. I believe Mary takes us by the hand and leads us to Jesus. When she stood at the foot of the cross with John, Jesus said to her, '*Woman, this is your son.*' And then he said to John, '*This is your mother.*'

Mary helps us to see ourselves as Jesus sees us. She can lead us through the crucifixion to the resurrection, which is self-forgiveness. Often we have to look at what we've done and, as Jean Vanier said, face the monsters within. I believe that the greatest way we can find self-forgiveness is by consecrating our heart to Mary. As St Louis de Monfort observed, this is when we truly give everything to Jesus and we never take them back.

My friend Jim, who had served time in prison for some serious offences, used to find it very difficult to show physical affection to his ten-year-old son. Because of his sins, he felt unworthy to give him a kiss or a hug. He didn't love himself, so he couldn't love his son. Instead he would give his son money.

He went on a pilgrimage to Medjugorje. One day, he visited the grave of Father Slavko, who had been a close friend of the "visionaries". He told me that while he was praying the rosary, Our Lady appeared to him. She said, *'Jim, why can't you forgive yourself. Two thousand years ago my son died so that you might be forgiven.'* He began to cry. When he walked away from the grave, for the first time in his life he could forgive himself. The first thing he did when he got back home was to take his son in his arms and hug him and tell him how much he loved him.

When I feel weak or broken because I've looked at the wrong pages on the internet or given in to lustful thoughts, I say to Mary, *'Help me to love myself. Help me not to condemn myself and to accept Jesus' mercy.'* She reassures me that these things are nothing compared to the forgiveness of God. I stop condemning myself and just pick myself up and give my sins to Jesus in confession and start again.

****
****

Something to think about

Do not let your hearts be troubled. Trust in God still, and trust in me.

John 14:1

Chapter 6

Getting Grief

When I was eleven years old, I came home one evening after attending Sea Scouts to find my mum and dad arguing. I'd never seen my dad look so angry. They ordered me upstairs, where I found my brother sobbing in their bed. He refused to tell me what Mum and Dad were arguing about, but mentioned a word I hadn't heard before: divorce.

A bit later, Mum and Dad came upstairs and sat on either side of the bed. '*Boys, you are going to have to choose who you want to live with,*' said Dad slowly and deliberately.

'*Why, Dad?*' I asked, unable to understand the question. '*Is this a game?*'

'*We're getting divorced,*' replied my mum with tears in her eyes.

Sometimes when we are hurt we can get angry with God for allowing us to suffer. When my parents decided to get divorced, my world fell apart. And I think I made a conscious decision back then not to love any more, because then I wouldn't get hurt.

Later in my life, after I'd found God, a priest once told me that I was angry with God, I denied it and said that I loved God. He shook his head and said, '*No, there's an anger in you against God because you wonder where he was in your childhood when you suffered.*'

'*Yes, where was God when I was getting beaten and being rejected?*' I found myself asking.

The priest replied, '*He was you. He suffered because you suffered. He was there in all your pain. So if you were hurt a lot, know that God also hurt a lot.*'

Questions about God and suffering are asked by people in every age. In the Bible, Job was someone who also wondered where God was in it. He wanted to know why he, an innocent man, was suffering so much. What had he done wrong?

'*My only food is sighs,*
and my groans pour out like water.
Whatever I fear comes true,
whatever I dread befalls me.
For me, there is no calm, no peace;
my torments banish rest.'

In 2005 my dad died. Yes, he suffered, but he accepted it and he also made his peace with God. I thank God that I was able to be at his bedside in hospital. During those last weeks of his life we grew closer. Our relationship hadn't always been close. But in those last weeks of his life I was able to see in a new way how much he loved me. And it was a great blessing to be able to pray with him. He was someone closer to God in his suffering than he probably imagined. After he'd watched a DVD of *The Passion of the Christ*, he said to me, *'John, I can now see that there's a reason for suffering. I know that I can unite my suffering to Christ and offer my pain up for others.'*

In his last days, Pope John Paul II showed to the world that a person still had dignity and value in suffering. He'd placed his life confidently in the hands of God. He showed us that there is no resurrection without the crucifixion.

Pope John Paul lived what he preached. During the Mass for the Anointing of the Sick at St George's Cathedral, Southwark, in 1982, he had said:

'Sickness and suffering seem to contradict all that is worthy, all that is desired by man. And yet no disease, no injury, no infirmity can ever deprive you of your dignity as children of God, as brothers and sisters of Jesus Christ. By dying on the cross, Christ showed us how to make sense of our suffering. In his passion we find the inspiration and strength to turn away from any temptation to resentment and grow through pain into new life. Suffering is an invitation to be more like the Son in doing the Father's will. It offers us an opportunity to imitate Christ who died to redeem mankind from sin. Thus, the Father has disposed that suffering can enrich the individual and the whole Church.'

What Jesus experienced on the cross has given meaning to suffering. He could have walked away but instead he embraced his suffering.

People often ask where God was in the Nazi concentration camps of the Second World War? Why did he allow so many millions to suffer? If he's a God of love, then why doesn't he intervene to stop suffering?

But God wasn't responsible for the millions who were tortured and died in the Nazi concentration camps. It was Man. God was present in the Nazi concentration camps.

He was in each man, woman and child as they were being crucified.

If a prisoner escaped from Auschwitz, the camp guards would select a prisoner and hang him. After a prisoner escaped one day, the guards selected three inmates, including a ten-year-old boy, and hung them. Usually, a prisoner's neck would break, but because the boy weighed so little his didn't. He hung there, slowly being strangled to death. The rest of the prisoners were made to file past the three victims.

As they did, a prisoner turned to a priest and sneered, *'Where is your God now?'*

The priest looked up at the little boy, but he wasn't there. In his place was Jesus dying on the cross.

'There he is, in the boy's place. Can you not see him?' said the priest.

When I was doing a parish mission in Dundalk a few years ago, I noticed a man in a wheelchair, and felt I should speak to him. He started to tell me about how he'd become an alcoholic and then started using drugs. This led to him becoming violent towards his wife and kids. He had a faith and, one day, he begged God to stop him from ruining his life and hurting his wife and kids.

Shortly after, he was driving in his van to work when he had a terrible crash, which left him paralysed from the waist down. *'You know, this was the greatest gift God ever gave me. I've been paralysed for nine years and in that time I've grown to love God and my wife and kids. It was only through God allowing me to have that accident that I stopped being an animal.'*

One time I was running a retreat at a school, a girl came up to me and said, *'Why does God allow suffering? Is it because people do things that are wrong?'*

'How do you mean?' I answered.

'Well, my mum has got cancer. Why has God allowed her to have cancer?'

'I don't believe for a moment that God wanted your mum to have cancer. Sickness was brought into the world through original sin. It wasn't what God planned. His plan was for us to have eternal life. But God suffers with your mum.'

'How?'

'He's in her pain and he's been hurt because she's been hurt. We might feel angry because he hasn't worked a miracle. But if he created too many miracles, we wouldn't have the freedom to choose. We'd be like robots. We'd all be worshipping and following him not because we chose to but because he made us do so.'

God has given each of us free will. We can choose to do good or evil. If we didn't have free will, we'd be robots. We would be programmed just to do good. The story of Adam and Eve in the book of Genesis shows us that Man was created in a state of knowing God and with free will. But Man chose evil and his nature was corrupted. This is called original sin. G.K. Chesterton once remarked, *'Whatever else is true of man, man is not what he was meant to be.'*

Pope Benedict XVI said, *'Faith has to be lived again and again in life and in suffering, as well as in the great joys that God sends us. It is never something that I can put in my pocket like a coin.'*

I sometimes think of Owen, who was bullied at school because of his stutter. He'd been to see speech therapists and psychologists, but they couldn't cure him. When he was seventeen his mum took him to a prayer group. He was prayed over and healed of his stutter.

At first he thanked God. But, as time went on, he drifted away from God. He started going to discos and going out with girls.

When he was twenty-two, he woke up one morning to find that his stutter had returned, although it wasn't as bad as it had been before. Terrified, he went to the church where he had been healed. He arrived to find a Mass going on.

In his homily, the priest talked about visiting Medjugorje. While he was there, he said, he'd watched in horror one day as a shepherd broke the legs of a lamb.

'What are you doing breaking the legs of this poor little lamb?' he asked.

The shepherd replied, *'This little lamb keeps on wandering away from me. If he keeps doing this, he's going to die. So I'm going to put his legs in splints and carry him on my shoulders.*

And he's going to learn to love me. He won't get lost and he won't die.'

Owen knew why God had given him the stutter back. He now thanks God every day for it.

When we travel through life we can be certain that, at some point, we will have to suffer. But we should realise that God is never the perpetrator. He's always the victim. He never inflicts the suffering on us. He always walks with us. In the darkest, most hurtful times of our life, that's when God is carrying us. And through the Passion he knows intimately what we suffer.

Father Slavko once told me about a twenty-year-old girl with multiple sclerosis who came to Medjugorje expecting to be cured. She hadn't really wanted to go, but her friends had persuaded her to do so. She wasn't cured though.

A year later, her friends decided to return to Medjugorje, and they asked her if she wanted to come with them. She agreed. The girl would sit in her wheelchair at the front of the church during the Masses. Father Slavko could see that she seemed very angry. At the Mass on the last day of her pilgrimage, he noticed that she no longer looked angry.

Afterwards, he went up to her and said, *'Something's happened to you. What is it?'*

'A year ago, Father, I came here and just wanted to be healed of my multiple sclerosis so that I would be able to walk. But God didn't heal me, so I became angry with him. When I came to Medjugorje again this year, I still felt angry and bitter when no cure happened. But yesterday I was touched by God in my heart and I have a peace and joy that is far better than being able to walk. Even though I haven't been cured, I've been healed in my heart. Now, I'm happy in my suffering. I know that I'm not alone. Jesus is with me.'

My friend Magnus, who runs the aid charity Scottish International Relief, told me the story of when he was visiting some street children in Colombia. He came across a six-year-old boy asleep on the floor. He picked up the boy and hugged him. As he did, the boy woke up.

'Where are your parents?' asked Magnus.

'I haven't got any parents,' replied the boy.

'Who looks after you?'

'God looks after me. He gives me everything.'

'How does he give you everything?'

'Last night before I went to sleep I prayed that I might receive a hug. And this morning I woke up in your arms.'

People often ask: where is God in suffering? It's better to ask: where are we when people like that little boy are suffering? What do we do to help? God worked through Magnus. And he works through each one of us, if we let him.

****

Something to think about

One night a man had a dream.
He dreamed he was walking along the beach with the Lord.
Across the sky flashed scenes from his life.
For each scene he noticed two sets of footprints in the sand:
one belonging to him, and the other to the Lord.
When the last scene of his life flashed before him,
he looked back at the footprints in the sand.
He noticed that many times along the path of his life
there was only one set of footprints.
He also noticed that it happened at the very lowest and saddest times in his life.
This really bothered him and he questioned the Lord about it.
"Lord, you said that once I decided to follow you,
you'd walk with me all the way.
But I have noticed that during the most troublesome times in my life,
there is only one set of footprints.
I don't understand why when I needed you most you would leave me.
"The Lord replied,"My son, my precious child,
I love you and I would never leave you.
During your times of trial and suffering,
when you see only one set of footprints,
it was then that I carried you."

Anonymous

Chapter 7

The Meet

I couldn't understand the importance of the sacraments when I first found God. After a spell in Pentonville Prison, where I'd served thirty days for not paying various fines, I attended a retreat. During the Blessed Sacrament procession, I asked someone what was happening. When he told me that little piece of bread was actually Jesus, I laughed and said that I thought this was ridiculous. *'I used to think that,'* said the guy, *'but I asked Jesus to show me that it was true. And he did.'*

So at Mass the next morning, I asked Jesus to show me that the bread I saw truly was him. At communion, I found myself automatically kneeling down. When I went back to my place, I experienced an incredible sensation, similar to what I'd experienced that night in my flat. It was a feeling a million times better than any joy I'd ever experienced. At this moment, I knew that Jesus was real in the Blessed Sacrament.

When you understand the Mass more you begin to see what a wonderful gift the Eucharist is. By taking on the appearance of bread and wine Jesus comes to us in a very special way.

Alan, a twelve-year-old boy who had been abused and lived in foster care, once came to a retreat I was helping to run. When the Blessed Sacrament was brought round he was totally overcome, and he threw himself in my arms, murmuring, *'I know I'm loved. I know I'm loved.'* A few months later he was baptised a Catholic, and I was made his godfather.

Six years later, he came with me to Feltham Young Offenders Institute in West London, which is known for the high number of suicides that have taken place amongst its inmates. At one point during my talk, I said to the lads, *'You know, it's okay for real men to show emotions.'*

When we came out, I noticed that Alan had tears in his eyes. I asked him if he was okay. He said, *'I thank God every day that you came into my school, or otherwise I know that I would be in a place like this.'*

Jean Vanier tells the story of the time he found a wheelchair tipped over at the bottom of the stairs leading to the chapel. He went inside and found Simon, a severely disabled young man, prostrate on the floor. He couldn't believe that the man had made such an effort to get into the chapel. Why did you do this? asked Jean Vanier. *'Because I wanted to be close to my friend,'* replied Simon.

Many young people say to me that the Mass is boring. If we watch a movie and are concentrating on something else at the same time, we lose interest. We have to pay attention to get something out of a movie. It's the same with Mass. If we concentrate on it, then we get something out of it.

Or it's like if you are a West Ham United fan and you go to Liverpool and Arsenal, you will get bored, because you're not interested in them. But if you go to watch West Ham, you're involved in every kick of the game. If you ask Jesus what he is saying to you in the readings at Mass and to let you know that he is truly present in the Eucharist, you start a personal relationship with him.

A priest friend of mine in Africa was once asked to say Mass in a remote village he'd never visited before. When he arrived, he was amazed to see an old woman caked in mud crawling along the ground. At communion, she crawled all the way to the front of the church, received Jesus and crawled back to her place.

Afterwards, he remarked to the sacristan, *'This is going to get really embarrassing. She is putting mud and filth all over the church.'*

'But, Father, she lost both of her feet through gangrene,' replied the sacristan.

Hearing this, the priest felt guilty, so he went to see the woman, who lived a mile from the church.

'I've got some great news for you. You don't have to crawl a mile to receive Jesus any more. I'm going to bring Jesus to you every Sunday,' he said.

'Please, Father, don't take away the privilege of me crawling to my saviour,' she pleaded.

Margaret Clitherow was someone who sacrificed her life for the Mass. She was brought up as a Protestant in York. At the age of fifteen she married a butcher and later became a Catholic. At this time in England, Catholics were under persecution and Mass had to be celebrated in secret by priests who moved around the country in fear of being caught and executed.

Margaret was soon helping and sheltering priests in the city, many of whom came from Douai in France. She knew that by helping to hide priests she was risking the death penalty. Although she was arrested several times under suspicion, the authorities found no evidence. Each time her home was raided, the priest managed to get away. Margaret and her family refused to answer any questions. However, one day a boy told the interrogators everything and Margaret was arrested, charged with harbouring priests and imprisoned in York Castle. She was pregnant at the time.

At her trial, the judge asked her to take the Bible in her hand and swear never to hide another priest. *'If you do this, you can go free,'* he said. *'But if not you will be taken outside and stripped naked. You'll then have a stone placed behind your back, a board put on top of you and boulders placed on it. Over three days you will slowly be crushed to death. The reason why the stone is placed behind your back is so that you will be in agony over these three days.'*

Margaret then asked for the Bible. *'I swear by Almighty God that if ever a priest needs hiding, I will hide him, because it's through his hands that I receive Jesus Christ.'*

She was then taken outside and, eventually, crushed to death. Her last words were *'Jesu! Jesu! Jesu! Have mercy on me.'*

At a school one time, I asked a group of girls if they really believed Jesus was present in the Eucharist. Many of the girls said that they didn't believe it. I noticed that one of the girls had what looked like slashes on her arms.

When it came to the girl whose arms had been slashed, she said, *'I used to think I was ugly and I hated myself. That's why I used to cut myself. But then I went to a retreat and as I went up to receive Jesus I said, "Show me that you love me. Show me that I'm beautiful." And I felt his love come into my heart. For the first time in my life I knew I wasn't ugly and that I was beautiful. So I stopped cutting myself. I wear short sleeves so that people* can *see that I've changed.'*

Archbishop Fulton Sheen used to spend an hour a day in front of the Blessed Sacrament. When he was asked why he did this he told the story of the time Communist soldiers came into a church in China and desecrated it, smashing the tabernacle and spilling the consecrated hosts all over the floor. They then beat up the priest and imprisoned him in the presbytery next door and placed soldiers around the church to prevent anyone from coming in.

All the priest could think about was an eleven-year-old girl who had hidden behind some pews when the soldiers came. He watched in amazement as she crawled out of her hiding place and went up to one of the hosts lying on the floor. After spending an hour in adoration, she picked up the host and placed it on her tongue. She then slipped past the guards and escaped.

The next day, he was even more amazed. The girl sneaked past the guards into the church, knelt down and spent an hour with Jesus. This went on for thirty-two days – there were thirty-two hosts on the floor. On the day she received the last host the soldiers caught her. In front of the priest they battered her to death with their rifle butts.

Archbishop Fulton Sheen said, *'If an eleven-year-old girl can give her life to Jesus then I'll spend an hour with Jesus each day for the rest of my life.'* And he did for fifty-five years.

In John's gospel Jesus said, *'Anyone who does eat my flesh and drink my blood has eternal life.'* If we do as Jesus says, he lives in us and we have life in us. J.R.R.Tolkein's eldest son once wrote to him to say that he felt he was losing his purpose in life. Tolkein wrote back and said that if there was one thing that he should place before everything in the world it is the Eucharist. This, he insisted, would always give him a purpose in his life.

When we receive Jesus in the Eucharist he gives us the strength to sustain us in our everyday life. In the sacrament of the Eucharist we – as humble and broken as we are – can receive Jesus, body, blood, soul and divinity, and draw life from him. We need that life and grace. That's why we should go to Mass as often as we can.

Father Adrian Crowley once told

me the story of the two curates who were being so badly treated by the parish priest that they decided to leave. Early one morning they packed their bags and crept out of the presbytery and into the church, which was the only way out to the street. As they were walking down the aisle, one of them said to the other, *'Let's just kneel and say a prayer.'* So they knelt down. After about an hour, one of them said, *'I can't leave him.' And the other said, 'I can't leave either.'* They could have left the priest, but they couldn't have left Jesus in the Blessed Sacrament.

At Mass, Jesus comes to us in a very special way. Malcolm Muggeridge once wrote about the Eucharist, *'Forgive me, Lord, for my pride and arrogance. It's all so simple. It's God coming in the form of bread.'* Our finite minds will never be able to grasp this mystery. We have to approach Mass in faith and humility.

My friend Neil once asked a group of kids at a school if they went to Mass. One girl said that she'd stopped going because her brother no longer went. She went on to say that since then Sundays had come to be quite empty and meaningless.

One Sunday morning, her grandmother asked her if she'd go to Mass with her, and she agreed. When they knelt down in the church she noticed her grandmother was crying.

'Are you okay, Gran?' she asked.

Her grandmother looked at her and said, *'I'm just so happy that you have come back to Mass because now you will receive Jesus.'*

****
****

Something to think about

In all truth I tell you,
if you do not eat the flesh of The Son of man
and drink his blood,
you have no life in you.

John 6:53

Chapter 8

Doing The Business

My life used to be about the unholy trinity of me, myself and I. I wasn't interested in anyone but myself. It's like in the film Sixth Sense when the little boy says, *'I see dead people.'* I was a dead person. This is what happens when you take and don't give. As a gangster, my life revolved around greed and selfishness.

Some years after my conversion I went on a pilgrimage to the Holy Land. One of the highlights was visiting the Dead Sea, which gets its name because it's below sea level. All the rivers flow into it and nothing flows out of it. All it does is take. It doesn't give. The locals say, *'If all you do in life is take and not give, then you're dead like the Dead Sea.'*

Not long after I found God, I felt a strong desire to give something back, so I decided to do some voluntary work at a drop-in centre based above a United Reformed Church in London. I collected pensioners in the mini-bus, began visiting those who were housebound and ended up cooking the Wednesday lunch. During my time there, I learned much about the importance of giving in the Christian life. But I probably received more than I gave.

It's in giving that we encounter Jesus. I often tell the kids I talk to in schools about when Father Bernard Murphy worked in a hospice in Calcutta, run by Mother Teresa. One day, she asked him to shave an elderly man. As he stood by the man, who had a bushy beard, a huge mop of hair and looked like a bag of bones, Father Bernard was overcome by an horrendous smell. Then he noticed that there were maggots crawling on the man's skin. Feeling repulsed, he began to shave him. The man couldn't speak but his eyes were saying, *'I love you for what you're doing.'* Sometime during the painful shaving process, the man turned into Jesus. Father Bernard went running over to Mother Teresa and said, *'I've just shaved the head of Jesus Christ.'*

Mother replied, *'When I was naked you clothed me, when I was hungry you fed me, when I was in prison you visited me, when I was thirsty you gave me a drink. Welcome to giving until it hurts. When you do it to the least of my brothers and sisters you do it to me.'*

Mother Teresa saw and worked miracles every day because she trusted completely in God. When a journalist visited her in Calcutta one time, she took him on a walk through the city. At the end of an alley was a leper. The journalist asked,

'Why did you go down the alley when we could have taken another route?'

'Because the Holy Spirit told me to,' replied Mother.

She then asked the journalist if he would carry the leper back to the house that she ran for those living on the streets.

'Will I catch something?' he asked.

'No, you won't catch anything,' she reassured him.

As he was wearing a white suit, he wasn't that keen on the thought of picking up the leper. But he did.

When they arrived at the house, he placed the leper on a bed. *'Now what do I do?'* he asked.

'Wash him,' instructed Mother.

He picked up the leper, lowered him into a bath in the middle of the floor, and then went to get a bucket and a cloth. When he turned around, he wasn't looking at the leper. He was looking at Christ. As he washed the man, all he could see was Jesus. When he emptied the bucket he saw that it was full of pieces of skin and pus. But when he looked at the man again, he was a leper once more.

As he was leaving the home, Mother Teresa appeared at the bottom of some steps. *'You saw him! You saw him!'* she exclaimed.

The greatest poverty, Mother Teresa said, was in the West, because although there was great wealth there was great spiritual emptiness. Jack Higgins, the best-selling novelist, admitted that if he only had known that fame and fortune was so meaningless and empty he never would have become a writer. And when tennis star Boris Becker won Wimbledon for the second time, he tried to commit suicide because his life was so meaningless, despite the wealth and fame that came to him. As a result of hitting rock bottom, he found Christ.

One time, Mother Teresa took some rice to a starving Muslim family. They were so undernourished that they looked like skeletons. She was amazed when the mother took a bowl, scooped some rice into it and went out the door. A few minutes later she returned with an empty bowl. Mother Teresa asked her where she had gone with the rice. The woman replied, *'My Hindu neighbour is also starving.'* At this, Mother Teresa began to cry. For the first time in her life she realised what it was to give until it hurt.

Father Glen Sudano, one of the Franciscan Friars of the Renewal in New York, once said to me that if we pray, go to Mass regularly and work with the poorest of the poor, then we are always close to God.

I used to help on a soup run in the West End of London. One night, I said to a dishevelled-looking guy, *'You should give up drinking, mate.'*

'I don't drink,' he replied.

'Well, you should give up drugs then,' I suggested.

'I don't take drugs.'

As my last throw of the dice, I said, *'Well, you should give up smoking.'*

He looked me in the eye and said, *'I don't smoke,'* and then added angrily, *'Do you know what you should give up?'*

'What?'

'You should give up judging people.' This taught me a big lesson. Before going out on the soup run, I'd thought all homeless people were druggies or drunks. That man humbled me.

I live off God's providence, which means I trust in God to provide. In 2004 I went on holiday to the United States. I spent some time in Florida, meeting Mickey Mouse and his friends and I also visited a priest friend of mine in Miami. I ended the holiday with a cruise to the Bahamas (God is very generous in his providence).

One evening, I was chatting to a barmaid and I decided to give her a Miraculous Medal. Immediately, she started to cry and then began to tell me that she was going through problems in her personal life. It turned out that this was her last night working on the ship.

'When I left Poland a year ago to come and work on this ship, someone at the airport gave me a rosary. But I left it in my suitcase. This morning, I took the rosary out and said a prayer to Our Lady to help me.'

I felt that the Miraculous Medal I'd given her was an answer to that prayer.

There's a story about six businessmen who were running along a platform at a railway station to catch a train to an important meeting. One of them bumped into a young boy selling apples on a stall, scattering the apples all over the floor, but they carried on running and jumped on the train.

Just as the train was leaving, one of the men jumped off and began to help the kid to pick up the apples. As he scooped up the apples, he noticed some of them were damaged.

Putting a few of the apples in his bag, he handed the boy some money. As he did, he realised the boy was blind. The boy looked at him and said, *'are you Jesus?'* He had prayed to Jesus to help him pick up the apples. The man who had helped him had been open to Jesus speaking to him.

I remember the time I was feeling exhausted after several months of giving talks in schools during the week and running retreats or parish missions at the weekend. We also had some tensions in the community. I was wondering what the point of it all was. Kneeling before Jesus in a church in Derry one evening during a reconciliation service, I prayed, *'Does what we do make a difference? Is there a point to it?'*

Just then I felt a tap on my shoulder. Looking round, I saw an elderly man standing there. *'There's a woman in the sacristy who wants to speak to you.'*

So I left the pew and made my way into the sacristy, where a smartly dressed woman was waiting.

'Hello,' I greeted her, wondering what she wanted.

'Is your name John Pridmore?'

'Yeah,' I nodded.

'Were you in a school in Claudy today?'

'Yeah, I was.'

'Well, my fifteen-year-old daughter tried to slash her wrists two weeks ago. She went back to school today and she wore a jumper to hide the stitches. She told me over forty-five minutes every single word you said in that school. At the end of it you said you can choose life in Jesus Christ or you can choose death, which is living without him.'

'That's right,' I said.

'She said to me, "Mum I choose life. I'm going to go back to Mass, pray the rosary with you and go to your prayer group." I saw my daughter die when she was twelve because she stopped praying and believing in God. And I saw her alive again today. You don't know how valuable what you are doing in schools is. Never stop it.'

Going back into the reconciliation service, I felt that God had answered my prayer. I then thought of something Mother Teresa had said when a journalist asked why she did what she did with the poor and dying in Calcutta. He said that what she did was only like a drip in a bucket. Mother Teresa replied that if everyone did the little bit that God asked them to do then the bucket would be overflowing and the world would be healed through love. As I knelt down, I told myself that if all my work over the last few years had only helped this one girl, then it was all worth it.

Archbishop Oscar Romero, who was gunned down in his cathedral in San Salvador while celebrating Mass, once said, *'All of us, if we really want to know the meaning of conversion and of faith and confidence in another, must become poor, or at least make the cause of the poor our own inner motivation. That is when one begins to experience faith and conversion: when one has the heart of the poor, when one knows that financial capital, political influence, and power are worthless, and that without God we are nothing. To feel that need of God is faith and conversion.'*

There's a story about a man who dies who arrives at the gates of heaven. St Peter looks at the book of life and says to him, *'You were incredibly rich, weren't you.'*

'Yes,' replied the man.

'But you never gave anything to anyone,' said St Peter.

'That's not true,' protested the man. *'I gave 20p to the Salvation Army once.'*

'Well, it's not written in the book,' said St Peter, and then he goes off to speak to St Michael.

'There's a multimillionaire outside who says that he once gave 20p to the Salvation Army, but it's not written in the book,' he said.

St Michael thought for a moment and then said, *'Okay – give him his 20p back and tell him to go to hell.'*

My friend Magnus MacFarlane-Barrow is someone doing incredible work with the world's poor. When he saw the TV images of innocent men, women and children suffering in the former Yugoslavia in 1991, he decided to do something about it. He and his brother, Fergus, put up posters in shop windows in their hometown of Dalmally, Argyllshire, asking for food, toiletries, toys and unwanted clothes. People responded generously and they filled a Land Rover with supplies and drove all the way to the former Yugoslavia to deliver them to the needy.

When Magnus visited a village in Malawi, he came across a woman dying of malnutrition.

'What can I do for you?' he asked.

'Feed my children,' she replied.

The next day, Magnus said to her eldest child, a fourteen-year-old boy, *'What do you want out of life? What do you dream of?'*

'I want a meal and I want to be able to go to school,' said the boy.

The words of this boy led to Magnus starting Mary's Meals, which provides daily meals for poor children around the world. It works through volunteers cooking the food. For doing this they receive a meal. Mary's Meals now feeds seventy-five thousand children a day.

There is no social justice when God is not at the centre of it. You can go to Africa and help the starving but if God is not in it it's meaningless. You are only really changing the world we live in if God is at the heart of what you do. Bob Geldof is hailed as a prophet-like figure by the media and others. But why? Okay, he's raising money, but he's not putting God at the centre of what he does. God asks us to change our lives and, like Mother Teresa, to give until it hurts.

****
****

Something to think about

For I was hungry and you never gave me food. I was thirsty and you never gave me anything to drink. I was a stranger and you never made me welcome, lacking clothes and you never clothed me, sick and in prison and you never visited me.

Matthew 25: 42–44

Chapter 9

Getting Tooled Up

Not long after I'd found God, I was backing my car out of the car park under the flats on the Cathall Road Estate, Leyton, when a Rastafarian in a Range Rover blocked my exit and refused to move.

'Come on mate. It's Christmas. Goodwill to all men and all that,' I shouted good-naturedly out of the window.

He didn't smile. Instead, he got out and started waving a baseball bat at me. There was no way I was backing down. Leaping out of my car, I opened the boot, whipped out my machete and stood there challenging him. He jumped straight back into the Range Rover and screeched away.

Turning my attention to God after being involved in so much violence and crime was a real battle at first. Over the years, I've learned that prayer is at the heart of our relationship with God.

Even now, I have to admit that I still go through periods of dryness, when I wonder if God hears me and if prayer really matters. But as someone once said, we should seek the God of consolations, not the consolations of God.

In the same way that a car needs petrol to run, we need prayer to function. I believe that if we don't pray, we become like animals. An African cardinal once asked a priest, *'Are you praying or have you become a dog?'* St Alphonsus said, *'If you pray, you will be saved; if you do not pray, you will be lost.'* Jesus expressed the same truth when he said, *'Cut off from me you can do nothing. A priest in Ireland I know put it another way. When I asked him why he prayed so much, he replied, "When I pray, I'm a nice person; when I don't pray, I'm horrible."'*

The best way I've found of beginning a prayer life with God is by going to confession. When we go to confession we take down the barriers we have erected through our sins. For me, confession or reconciliation, has been a source of terrific healing and grace. God's forgiveness is there for us again and again and again. The popular Divine Mercy devotion, which Pope John Paul II advocated, speaks only of God's unending mercy for us.

One of my spiritual directors asked me, *'Do you like the highs, John?'*

'Yes, I love them,' I replied.

'Do you like the lows?'

'No, I hate them,' I admitted.

'Well, then, get a balance,' he said.

He meant that we shouldn't go too high and we shouldn't go too low.

Because time is God's I believe that when we waste time with God we have time for everything else. Robert Toone, a barrister friend of mine, once told me that before he does any work he always prays. If he doesn't pray, he never gets the work finished. Spending time in prayer creates time.

How much time do we spend each week watching TV, listening to CDs or going out with our mates? We could get up earlier or go to bed later.

Two men once went to meet Mother Teresa. When the first asked her how much he should pray, she asked him what was his job.

'I'm retired,' he said.

'Pray one hour a day,' she advised.

'How much should I pray?' asked the second man.

'What do you do?' she asked.

'I'm a stockbroker,' he answered.

'Pray two hours a day,' she urged. *'Why should I pray two hours a day when you have recommended that my friend prays just one hour a day? He has a lot more free time than me. I work ten hours a day, five days a week, plus weekends sometimes.'*

She looked at him and said, *'The busier you are the more you need to pray.'*

A friend of mine told me about the time he came home from school to discover that his mother had been diagnosed with inoperable cancer. In other words, she was dying. Distraught, he left the house and went to his local church. It was the first time he'd been into a church in years. He knelt before a statue of Mary and prayed, *'You know what it is to have a son love you. And I love my mum. I ask you to beg your son to heal my mother. If you do, I'll pray a rosary every day for the rest of my life.'* He then lit a candle and left.

Two weeks later his mother went to the hospital for tests. The cancer had disappeared. The doctors thought they had made a mistake. But my friend knew that Mary had interceded for his mother, so he started praying the rosary every day, as he promised.

After a few months, he remembered that when he was young his mother had taught him the Hail Mary to help him get over his fear of the dark. But when he'd overcome that fear he'd stopped praying it. He realised this healing of his mum was a reminder not to forget his promise to pray the rosary every day. He's now forty and he prays the rosary daily.

We live in two worlds, the physical one which we can see, and the spiritual world, which is invisible. In our very materialistic world it can sometimes be hard to see that there's a spiritual world. I once went into a cafe in the East End. It was packed, so I squeezed alongside an old woman. I got talking to her about this and that. It was clear she had fallen on hard times, so I suggested that the Society of St Vincent de Paul might be able to help her. When she got up to leave, I gave her a rosary, and her eyes lit up. Now, if that cafe hadn't been so full I wouldn't have ended up talking to that woman about God.

Another time, I was at a retreat. Standing in front of me was a young lad, and when the priest called on the Holy Spirit, he fell over backwards. I thought his head was going to hit the stone floor, but it hit my foot. If my foot hadn't been there, his head would have been split open. God knew that he was going to be slain in the Spirit and he put my foot in exactly the place where his head was going to fall.

God's language is always silence. You can't have peace without prayer. I've tried every way of getting out of prayer. But I've realised that if I don't pray, I don't have peace in my life. I think of prayer as wasting time with God.

When the best-selling writer Scott Peck was asked on TV by Oprah Winfrey how he managed to write so many books, give lectures and travel the world, he replied, *'I spend two hours in prayer every day.'*

She said, *'I'm not asking you what you do. I'm asking you how you fit in everything.'*

'That is how I fit in everything,' he said. *'Because I give those two hours to God, I have time to do everything else God wants me to do.'*

After St Francis of Assisi found God he said the same prayer for three years: who are you, Lord, and who am I?

I remember the time Winifred, an elderly lady I used to visit, was dying in hospital. When I gave her a rosary, she said, *'I know what this is. It's Our Lady's hand, and she will take me to her son.'* In the Hail Mary we pray, *'Holy Mary, Mother of God, pray for us sinners now and at the hour of our death.'* An hour after I gave Winifred the rosary she died.

One of the ways God spoke to me so powerfully after I found him was through the Bible. The first Bible I was given was a King James Version, which had the words of Jesus written in red. And the first story I ever read was the parable of the prodigal son. As I read it, I knew that it was speaking about me. The Bible is the word of God and it's a living word. It's not dead. And it can speak to us in a thousand ways through prayer and meditation.

In the community I live in we pray the Divine Office each morning, evening and night. The office is built around the psalms, which are a wonderful way of praising God. When we pray the Office we know that we are praying with millions of other Catholics around the world. Like the rosary, the Office is a tool of prayer.

When I first started reading it, I found some of it, especially the Old Testament, difficult to understand.

Scott Hahn, in his book *A Father Who Keeps his Promises*, writes, *'After spending a decade intensively studying Scripture, I had finally begun to see the "big picture" of salvation history, and how all of the innumerable puzzle pieces fit together into a big, beautiful divine love story. All the many names, places and events in Scripture often leave first-time readers feeling overwhelmed and bewildered. Honestly, it took me years before I formed a "mental map" to find my way around Scripture, especially the Old Testament, without getting lost. But once I mapped out the peak events of the mountain range of salvation history, I finally got the big picture.'*

I see the Old Testament as a bit like

a father teaching a child – Israel – what it is to be obedient. In the New Testament Israel becomes a man and sees its salvation in Jesus.

As Scott Hahn says, you have to see the bigger picture with the Old Testament. Running through it is a golden thread of the chosen people journeying towards God. Even though they often turn away from God, he never rejects them. Someone once said that the Psalms teach us how to pray; Job teaches us how to suffer; the Song of Songs teaches us how to love; Proverbs teaches us how to live; and Ecclesiastes teaches us how to enjoy.

The fulfilment of the Old Testament is the New Testament, because that's when salvation came to earth, through Jesus. As an old saying puts it, the New Testament lies hidden in the Old and the Old Testament is unveiled in the New.

I take consolation from the fact that the Bible is full of sinners. When I lived in the presbytery of St Joan of Arc in Highbury, North London, some of the parishioners were up in arms about me because I was an ex-gangster. Father Fred, the parish priest, gave a talk one night and talked about how God used flawed human beings. He told the parishioners that Moses was a murderer, David an adulterer, that Peter denied Christ three times and that Paul had persecuted the first Christians. That God can do extraordinary things through people so broken gives me great encouragement when I become conscious of my own sins.

In *The Bible Jesus Read*, Philip Yancey says, '*The Old Testament portrays the world as it is, no holds barred. In its pages you will find passionate stories of love and hate, blood-chilling stories of rape and dismemberment, matter-of-fact accounts of trafficking in slaves, honest tales of the high honour and cruel treachery of war. Nothing is neat and orderly. Spoiled brats like Solomon and Sampson get supernatural gifts; a truly good man like Job gets catastrophe. As you encounter these disturbances, you may recoil against them or turn away from a God who had any part in them. The wonderful quality of the Old Testament is that it contains those very responses as well! God anticipates our objections and includes them in his sacred writing.*'

People wonder why God sometimes seems vengeful in the Old Testament. I'd say that because God's chosen people had a natural anger towards their enemies they sometimes portrayed God as vengeful. It's important to read the Old Testament in the context of the time it was written in, not from a twenty-first century viewpoint. The ancient world was very different from today: there was no TV, iPods, cars or planes. It's easy to forget this. God can be angry, but his is a just anger.

The Old Testament is vital in understanding Jesus. He was a Jew and grew up and ministered in a Jewish culture. From his childhood, he would have been steeped in the Old Testament. And, of course, he was the fulfilment of it. A friend who used to be an Orthodox Jew once shared a flat with a girl who was a Christian. When he heard her praying in tongues one day, he walked into her room and asked her why she was praying that prayer.

'I'm not praying any prayer,' she replied. *'I'm praying in tongues.'*

He said, *'No, you're praying in perfect Hebrew.'*

This made him intrigued and he started reading the New Testament, something Orthodox Jews aren't allowed to do. As he read it, he realised that everything Jesus revealed was the fulfilment of what he had been waiting for all his life.

We shouldn't worry about dryness in prayer. When I first found God I experienced immense consolation. Every time I prayed I felt filled with the Holy Spirit. And when I went to Mass the gospel would be alive to me. It seemed as if God was speaking directly to me. But as time went on this consolation disappeared and prayer and Mass began to be dry. I began to wonder if I'd done something wrong to make God leave me. But, after speaking to my spiritual director, I realised that I hadn't done anything wrong. He told me that God often gives people consolation at the beginning of their faith journey and then takes it away. It's his way of saying, *'will you still follow me without the consolation?'* It's a test of our faith and means that we are drawing closer to God.

When Mother Teresa was asked when was the last time she experienced God's consolation she replied, *'I can't remember. It was so long ago.'* She went through a dark night of the soul for forty years, yet her faith remained strong.

In order to pray, it's important to be still. And in our busy, noisy world this can be difficult. Scott Peck told the story of a priest who said he was working sixteen hours a day and had no time. Scott Peck told him to go home and spend an hour in silence and invite God into his life. The priest agreed to do this and went away. A week later, he returned. When Peck asked him how he had got on, he said he got bored, so he put a Mozart record on.

'I didn't ask you to listen to Mozart,' said Peck, *'I asked you to sit in silence with God for an hour.'*

'But this would drive me mad,' said the priest.

'You couldn't sit with yourself for an hour a day and yet you will inflict yourself on other people for sixteen hours a day,' replied Peck.

The gospels tell us that when Jesus prayed he often went away to a lonely place. It's important to find somewhere where you can be alone and in silence. This might be a church, your room, or a local park. We need to create space for God and to listen to him. It's hard to do this when we are surrounded by noise and activity.

We have to pray how we feel. If we are feeling at peace, we should tell God. If we feel angry, then we should tell God we're angry, because this gives him the opportunity to remove the anger.

Not everyone finds it easy to praise God. Yet we live in an age where celebrities have praise heaped upon them. We have much to praise God for: our life, health, family, friends, talents, food, nature. I think praise is one of the keys in the spiritual life. St Augustine says that the only thing we can do for God which has no fault, is praise. Everything else we can do can have faults. When I wake up, the first thing I say is, *'thank you, Lord, for this beautiful day.'*

I remember leading a retreat at Ampleforth Abbey and going into the chapel on my own one evening. As I sat there, I was just babbling away and not speaking from the heart. Suddenly, I just stopped and thanked Jesus for being there in the good times and the bad times and for his faithfulness.

One of the things I've found in my own life is that when I pray to know God more and understand his plan for me, he answers me. But if I pray for material things that I don't really need he doesn't answer me.

Sometimes I feel that I can't pray. It might be because I don't know what words to use, or because I feel exhausted or sinful. When I feel like this, all I say is *'Jesus, I rest my head on your heart, like John the beloved did at the Last Supper.'* And I always feel that Jesus holds me. It isn't how we pray. It's how honest we are in prayer. The more honest we are with ourselves and with God, the more God can answer our prayers. I don't believe it's about receiving instant answers. It's about opening our hearts to his will. And he lets us know his will in ways and means that we couldn't understand.

When St John Vianney asked an old man, who used to sit in his church for hours on end, what he did in church all that time, he replied, *'I look at him; and he looks at me.'*

****
****

Something to think about

I never have the satisfaction of feeling I have prayed, not even the certainty that I have been faithful. I have no certainties at all about myself except that I am loved by God and God's love can be relied upon to purify, transform me and finally complete the work.

Sister Ruth Burrows

Chapter 10

What Are You Looking At?

When I was involved in organised crime, I had no shortage of women who wanted to have sex with me. Most of the clubs I worked in were like glorified meat markets. I frequently gave into my lust and woke up the following morning in bed with a woman whose name I could barely remember.

When I once asked Winifred, who had been happily married for forty-five years, why she felt so many marriages today failed, she replied, *'Me and my husband courted for two years before we got engaged. We didn't get married until two years later. We knew each other very well and he became my best friend. Nowadays, people just jump into bed with each other and don't get to know each other as friends.'*

Winifred was right. For many people today relationships are about emotions rather than God; about sex rather than genuine love.

In 1967 when Pope Paul VI published his encyclical *Humanae Vitae*, which taught that only natural family planning was part of God's plan, he was condemned from all sides. Even some priests spoke out publicly against him, saying that he was out of touch. One of the consequences of contraception, Pope Paul said, would be widespread infidelity in marriage. He's been proved right, if the divorce courts are anything to go by.

Pope John Paul II was also attacked for preaching against what he called 'the culture of death', meaning abortion, contraception and sexual promiscuity. He was like an Old Testament prophet, warning people of the consequences of sexual immorality.

During the first five years of his pontificate, Pope John Paul developed 'the theology of the body' in the weekly talks he gave. This was an attempt to explain that the Church's teaching on sexual ethics was not out of date, but was in tune with the modern world and its search for freedom and fulfilment. He showed the Church does not reject the body. By taking human flesh, God made the body sacred.

He said, *'The body, in fact, and it alone is capable of making visible the invisible: the spiritual and the divine. It was created to transfer into the visible reality of the world, the mystery hidden since time immemorial in God, and thus to be a sign of it.'*

The Catholic Church is often criticised for refusing to allow condoms to be used in the fight against Aids. But to give someone who has Aids a condom is giving them a false sense of security. It's encouraging them to think that they can have safe sex. There's no such thing as safe sex. In reality, a lot of people catch Aids because they think condoms are safe.

I remember a woman on a TV programme going on about why kids today should use condoms. An old lady in the audience then said, *'When I was a teenager we didn't have all these problems with teenage pregnancies and sexually transmitted diseases because we abstained from sex. The only safe way I know of not getting pregnant or catching a sexually transmitted disease is saving the act of sex for marriage. And then it's making love, not having sex.'*

When a cardinal in Africa was accused by a journalist of being responsible for people dying of Aids, he asked *'why?'* The journalist replied, *'because the Catholic Church wouldn't let people use condoms'.*

'Abstinence, not sex, is the solution to the problem of Aids,' refuted the cardinal.

'But you can't expect adults not to have sex,' retorted the journalist.

'Why? Are they loved children of God or are they dogs?' retorted the cardinal.

I often tell a story of a girl who lived in a village and longed to be loved. She met a guy and ended up sleeping with him. But afterwards she didn't feel fulfilled, so she split with him. She met another guy and slept with him. Again, she didn't feel fulfilled, and the relationship ended. Then she met another guy and the same thing happened. The reason she ended up sleeping with the first guy that came along was because she hoped she would feel loved and valued. Then she decided that she might as well get paid for sleeping around, so she became a prostitute.

One day, she was in a house when a man she hadn't seen before walked in. The minute she saw him she knew that he would make her feel loved. And the tears streamed down her face. She was so overcome that she fell down at his feet and dried the tears with her hair.

The man looked at her and said, *'Even though your sins are many you are forgiven because you have loved much.'* She had met Jesus. And the first person Jesus appeared to after his resurrection was Mary Magdalene.

We're surrounded by sexual images wherever we go, and this can make chastity difficult. I used to struggle with masturbation. To overcome this I asked for God's grace and for the gift of chastity. The fact is that when you masturbate you place yourself in a powerful position because it is a fantasy, an illusion. It makes a person an object rather than someone made and loved by God. Masturbation is a selfish act which corrupts this gift from God. We shouldn't use people as objects. This is what animals do. When we use others as sexual objects we are never fulfilled. It leaves us feeling empty. I still struggle with masturbation and I still fall. But when I do fall, I place myself at the merciful heart of Jesus.

I once asked an old priest, *'When does lust stop, Father?'* He replied, *'When the last nail goes into the coffin.'*

The Church's teaching that homosexual and lesbian activity is sinful has led to it coming under fire from many sections of society. Some people say, *'What does it matter whether you're attracted to someone of the opposite sex or your own sex?'* The answer is simple: homosexual and lesbian sex is against natural law and is condemned by God. In fact, in nearly every culture and religion it's been seen as unnatural. And we now have same sex partnerships – gay marriages – legalised in some countries.

God doesn't reject a person because of their sexuality, however. His love and grace is there for all. The Catechism distinguishes between homosexuality and homosexual acts. As St Augustine said, *'Love the sinner, but hate the sin.'*

There are those today who maintain that a person is born homosexual, so they can't change. In the US, Courage ministers to men and women with same sex attractions. It follows the teaching of the Church and its approach is based on prayer, the sacraments and friendship. It's helped many men and women with their struggles to be chaste, and it's helped many turn away from same sex relationships.

Its web site has some powerful testimonies on it.

I once heard a story about a very promiscuous homosexual who was sent to prison for having sex with a rent boy. One night, Jesus appeared to him in his cell and said, *'The only arms that you need around you are mine.'* That was a turning point for him. He renounced homosexuality and began to live a chaste life.

Teenagers often e-mail me about problems they have with their sexuality. Society's message that homosexual activity is normal can create conflict in some teenagers. One fifteen-year-old lad told me that he wanted to kill himself because he felt he was homosexual and couldn't live with this. I explained that it was normal at puberty to sometimes go through an attraction to someone of the same sex. But I told him that we have to turn away from this. If we embraced it, it might become second nature. But if you don't act on it, you can grow out of it. When I tell young people that just because they experience an attraction to someone of the same sex doesn't mean they are gay, it's like a breath of fresh air for them.

Society trivialises the word love. It talks about making love and falling in love. When I talk about the love of God I mean unconditional love. It's easy to think we're in love when it is just strong emotions or lust.

We need to be honest with ourselves and honest with God. We can't grow spiritually unless we are honest. A woman I once knew invited me around to her house one night. She was a single mum, and I knew that she wanted male company. I was looking forward to seeing her. But on my way there I asked God why I was going. I instantly knew the reason was lust. I prayed for grace not to give in to it. I didn't and we are still friends today. I might have ended up sleeping with her had I not been honest with myself and asked God to help me.

Struggles with lust should not keep us from prayer. God understands our weaknesses. There's a story about a man carrying a sack on a long journey. The further he travelled, the heavier the sack became, until he could walk no further because of its weight. In the distance he saw a raging sea. Standing on the seashore was a man dressed in white with blood running from his hands and feet. When he got closer, the man in white said to him, *'Give me your burden, my son.'* Using the last of his energy, the traveller passed him the sack. The man in white threw the sack into the sea. Immediately the sea became calm, and a big sign that said 'No fishing' appeared on the surface. The man's sack represents his sins, the sea represents the storm in his soul. When Jesus takes his sins, immediately his soul goes calm. The *'No fishing'* sign means that when we give Jesus our sins they no longer exist, so leave them in the past.

We live in a society where lust and sex are portrayed as the norm. I think Jesus understands how hard it is for us to keep a pure heart and be chaste. He's offering us more and more grace, as the world becomes more and more sexual. If we allow him to give us this grace, he will protect us. We need to ask him each day to be pure in heart, mind, body and soul. And when we are in relationships we have to try with all our heart to keep them free from emotional ties. Our sexuality is a gift, but it's one that should only be used in the sacrament of marriage.

During a trip to America in 2002 I met a girl called Stacey. Immediately there was a spark between us and a strong friendship soon developed. She was a very committed Catholic and we used to pray together and talk about what God was doing in our lives. I knew that in the past my sex drive had led me into unholy relationships, so, when we started going out together, I told her that we needed to establish some boundaries.

I thought that Stacey and I were meant to get married, so we got engaged. But, through prayer and reflection, I discerned that God wasn't calling us to be together. The break-up was painful, but it would have been more painful if we'd let emotions dominate our relationship. And because emotions were not clouding my judgement, I could see what God wanted.

Long engagements are a good idea to test a relationship. A couple need to become best friends. Yet, some people know in a short space of time that they have met the right person and if what they have between them is genuine love. But this is rare.

It's not fashionable nowadays to talk about sin. What used to be called sinful behaviour is often now held up by the media and society as good behaviour. Think of the antics on TV programmes such as Big Brother, or the way some celebrities are almost applauded in the tabloids for their sexual behaviour.

When you watch TV you find that what used to be called sin is often ridiculed. I remember back in the 1980s when Freddie Starr started off a show with a stream of expletives. There was uproar. Now though, expletives are used in many programmes and films. I find this sad because I believe swearing reveals something about a person's spirit. And of course, now on TV you not only have expletives in many programmes but also explicit sexual scenes that are little different to porn.

It's the same with music. So many songs are littered with sexual innuendo and talk about 'making love'. I remember once being in McDonald's and complaining to the manager about the rap song they were playing. It was full of expletives. He was shocked when he realised this. He'd been so busy that he hadn't noticed the words to the song. He immediately asked one of the staff to turn the music off.

Society tells us that whatever sexual feelings we have we should act on them. If we do, we'll experience freedom. In my past, the more I acted on my sexual desires the more I became a prisoner. The more I become free from my sexual desires and embrace the grace of God's offering, the more I become truly free.

I know someone who fell in love with a guy when she was fifteen. Because she loved him, she did as he wanted and had sex with him. Within a few weeks, he dumped her. She felt it was like a part of her heart being ripped out. She then met another guy and when he asked if they could have sex, she gave in again. This relationship, too, ended soon after. She then began sleeping around.

Eventually she did meet a guy who she really loved and wanted to marry. Reflecting back on those other relationships, she said to me, *'I wish that I hadn't got into them. I feel they took away a part of my soul.'*

A girl who used to come to me for spiritual direction told me that she was sexually abused as a child by someone outside the family. As a result, she started sleeping around. On one occasion, when she was sixteen, she had sex with five guys at the same time. Soon after, she tried to kill herself.

I said to her, *'Place yourself back in the situation and I'm going to invite Jesus in.'*

While I was praying over her, she began to cry uncontrollably. When she eventually stopped, I asked her what happened.

'Jesus just put this white cloak around me and kept on saying, "My beautiful, innocent seven-year-old child."'

Jesus didn't see her as promiscuous. All he could see was a seven-year-old girl who had been abused. She realised that she wasn't responsible and that she shouldn't condemn herself. She saw that she needed to love herself.

We should never judge ourselves. We should just give ourselves to God and ask him to be our judge and allow his forgiveness to flood through us.

****
****

Something to think about

Love is always patient and kind; love is never jealous; love is not boastful or conceited, it is never rude and never seeks its own advantage, it does not take offence or store up grievances. Love does not rejoice at wrongdoing, but finds its joy in the truth. It is always ready to make allowances, to trust, to hope and to endure whatever comes. Love never comes to an end.

1 Corinthians 13: 4-7

Chapter 11

Putting Manners On You

I used to believe that what would make my life whole were drugs, power and money, the things the world said that would make me complete and happy. The reality was that I found those things to be meaningless and empty. I'd looked for forgiveness in all the wrong places and I had a false sense of wholeness.

When I found God I understood what wholeness really was. Shortly after my conversion, I gave away my money and started doing voluntary work. On my way to Mass each day, I'd have a laugh with some of the criminals on the estate where I lived, and I'd ask them if they wanted to come to church with me.

But then I felt in prayer that I was sinning and not glorifying God, so I decided not to speak to anyone. This way, I wouldn't sin. After a week of this silence, I went to my mum's one evening for a meal.

My step-dad said to me, *'John, what's going on? I haven't heard you say a word all week.'*

'Well, every time I opened my mouth I was sinning.'

'You know all those guys you used to have a laugh with?'

'Yeah?'

'Well, they think they've upset you. John, God made you a happy–go-lucky cockney. That's who you are. Yes, you're going to make mistakes, but this will make you holy in God's eyes. Say you're sorry and just keep on walking. Use the personality God gave you. Never try and change who you are.'

What my step-dad said changed my idea of holiness dramatically. Father Harold Brock once said to me, *'The difference between the saints and us is that the saints had holes in them, just like us, but they used Jesus to fill the holes.'*

Father Bob Faricy told me that he used to be addicted to gambling. Through the grace of God, he was able to stop. Yet he still had the desire to gamble. He was in Monte Carlo one time, and he heard the Holy Spirit tell him to go into a casino and bet on number 36 at the roulette table. So he placed a hundred dollars on it. It came up and he won over three thousand dollars. Then he heard the Holy Spirit say, *'Do whatever you want.'* So he gambled all the money and lost it all, apart from a hundred dollars. As he walked out, he felt the Holy Spirit say, *'I'm in charge of everything.'* And after that, he never had the desire to gamble again.

Many times in my life I looked at the stories about the saints, and they seemed to float down from heaven, dance with daffodils, and then seemed to float back up to heaven. But the reality is that they went through anguish and pain as well as joy. Each of them was born with original sin and struggled to be what God wanted them to be. The last words of St Louis de Montfort were, *'I have Jesus on my right hand and Mary on my left, and you have no more hold over me.'* He was talking to the Devil. He knew that he was still a sinner. In the same way, on his death bed, St Francis of Assisi begged his community to pray for him, so that he wouldn't go to hell.

We often read the lives of the saints in a distorted way, where we think holiness is perfection. It's not. Holiness is wholeness in God, complete and utter peace with him. When I found God, I realised that there were some bad traits in my personality. I had been sadistic at times. But God has now removed this from my heart. He changes us from the inside out.

We don't have to be afraid to make mistakes. We have to be afraid not to give those mistakes to God and ask him to heal us in those areas where we struggle. Father Slavko once said, *'It's no good looking at our faults and failings without looking at the cross.'* When we look at our faults and failings through the redemption of the cross, it's like God places his hand on the roots of our sins. He pulls up the roots and the weeds die. If we don't pull up the roots, the weeds won't die. If we allow Jesus to pull up the roots in us, we will become truly whole.

During my time with the Franciscan Friars of the Renewal we used to kneel in the chapel for three hours, not to impress God but to impress each other. It's easy to fall into this trap of perfection. It's God who makes us perfect. We can't make ourselves perfect.

I once visited the cell in Auschwitz where a Polish soldier had been imprisoned. Because he'd tried to get the other prisoners to rise up against the guards, he'd been tortured more than anyone else.

There, etched on the wall, was an image of the Sacred Heart of Jesus and one of the crucified Christ. Underneath, in Polish, he had written, Never without hope.' As I walked away, it really hit me that this man knew how to suffer and become holy in Christ.

I also visited the cell of St Maximilian Kolbe, a Franciscan priest who was sent to Auschwitz for speaking out against the Nazis. While he was there, he gave his rations to other prisoners who were facing starvation.

One day, after a prisoner escaped, the guards chose ten men to be starved to death as a reprisal. One of them fell to his knees and begged the commanding officer not to be taken because he was married and had children.

St Maximilian stepped forward and said. *'Let me take his place.'*

The commanding officer agreed, and St Maximilian and nine other men were stripped and taken to an underground bunker and left without food or water. When the guards checked the bunker they found the men were not howling in agony, as was usually the case, but singing and praying. Eventually eight of the prisoners died, leaving alive St Maximilian and one other man. St Maximilian was given a lethal injection and burned in the oven the next day. The other man survived Auschwitz, and when St Maximilian was canonised in 1982 he was present at the ceremony.

When St Therese of Lisiex was dying in the convent infirmary, one of the sisters found her awake and gazing towards heaven.

'What are you doing? You ought to be trying to sleep,' said the sister.

'I can't, Sister, I am suffering too much for that, so I pray.'

'What do you say to Jesus?'

'Nothing. I just love him.'

All the saints urge us to make little sacrifices. For instance, it might be not taking that cream cake when you really want it. They also encourage fasting. Jesus says that there are certain evil spirits that can only be driven away through fasting. I think we've forgotten the importance of fasting today.

St John Vianney said the two greatest sacrifices we can give to God are fasting from food and fasting from sleep. In my community in Ireland we all get up at 3a.m. to say the Divine Mercy Prayer. Leaving a warm bed isn't easy sometimes, I'll admit, but when we want real miracles to happen in our lives, then we need to make sacrifices.

In our community we have a weekly examination of conscience. This plays a key part in sorting out problems that any of us might have with each other. If someone says sorry for something they have done, then usually others will do the same. It's often our weakness rather than power, that changes people.

An examination of conscience helps us in conversion, because we see who we really are and we also see ourselves through the eyes of others. The more open we are to seeing ourselves deep in our brokenness, the more open we are to true conversion and holiness in God.

Getting to know God takes a lifetime. This is just the same as getting to know anyone. To know God you have to waste time with him in prayer.

****
****

Something to think about

Let the Word of Christ, in all its richness, find a home in you.

Colossians 3:16

Chapter 12

Cop On

When I was engaged to Stacey, I began to wonder where God was calling me. Should I marry her, move to the United States and become a youth minister in a parish, as Stacey wanted me to do? Or should I continue living as a single man, relying on God's providence and be an evangelist? Over the next few weeks, I prayed each day about this, asking God to give me guidance.

After leading a confirmation programme at a retreat centre in the Wirral, I sat in my car and prayed for guidance. What did God want me to do with my life? Did he want me to carry on being an evangelist? I didn't know. I turned on the ignition key and put on a tape called *Revival in Belfast* by Robert Mark, which someone had left in the car. As I waited for a set of traffic lights to change, I heard the words *'When it's all been said and done / There's just one thing that matters / Did I do my best to live for truth? Did I live my life for you?'* I knew that God had answered my prayer: he wanted me to be an evangelist.

Soon after, at the New Dawn Conference at Walsingham, I asked my friends Neil and John what they both thought I should do with my life. I trusted both their judgements. Neil and I had run missions together and John was training for the priesthood. They both thought I should be an evangelist. God speaks to us through other people. He had used Neil and John to tell me what he wanted to do.

Discernment is an important part of the Christian life. By discernment, I mean finding out what God wants us to do. Father Bob Faricy has a great way of discerning what God wants. For example, if he was about to buy a car, he'd sit in the chapel for two minutes and say, *'I'm going to buy this particular car,'* and see how this feels. He will then say *'I'm not going to buy the car,'* and see how that feels. He makes his decision on the peace he feels. If he feels anxious about a decision he is thinking of making, then he won't do it. The bigger the decision, the more time he would spend in prayer.

When I was thinking of leaving the Franciscan Friars of the Renewal in The Bronx, I prayed for a month. Afterwards, I felt I should leave. This gave me an incredible peace. In the second month I prayed about staying, and I felt a lot of inner turmoil and anguish.

I once entered religious life and I was once engaged to be married. It was God who closed these doors, not me. I now feel strongly that God has called me to live as a lay single person.

At the end of 2004 I felt I really needed a holiday, somewhere hot but also cheap. It had been a busy year of talks and missions. I told a friend of mine and he searched on the internet for somewhere. He found a weeklong package deal in a five-star hotel in Egypt for about two hundred quid. I couldn't believe it was so cheap. But he checked and the price was correct. I wondered if the appeal of the holiday could be the Devil trying to distract me. I prayed about it and felt that God did want me to go.

So I booked the trip, but wondered if my discernment was right. Was I deceiving myself into thinking God wanted me to spend a week in a five- star hotel in Egypt? A couple of days later I received a cheque for £500 from a friend of mine. He said, *'Take yourself away on a nice holiday.'* I knew then that this was a sign from God.

Discernment is a long process. We're not good at it after a year. It takes a lifetime to know whether it is God's voice we are hearing, our own or that of the world. We never reach our true understanding of discernment until we are standing before God. Fear can sometimes prevent us from being open to God's grace. In the gospel we read about how the disciples were in a boat with Jesus on the Sea of Galilee and became frightened when a storm broke out. Jesus asked them why they had so little faith. I always take heart from the fact that the disciples, who lived with Jesus and knew him intimately, still lacked faith. I know in my life when I've been frightened, I've been frightened of an illusion. In his letter to the Romans, Paul said, *'Where sin increased, grace increased all the more.'*

Mary was frightened when the angel appeared to her, yet she freely opened herself to God and through her he brought about our salvation in Jesus. We are called to do the same as Mary: allow God's grace to work in our lives. He gives it freely to us and if we accept it into our lives we can be radically transformed into what God wants us to be. In the words of the Catechism of the Catholic Church, *'Grace is a supernatural gift of God, freely bestowed on us for our sanctification and salvation.'*

The writer Flannery O'Connor wrote, *'All human nature vigorously resists grace because grace changes us and the change is painful.'* I know this is true from my own experience. Leaving behind my former life as a gangster to follow Christ wasn't easy. It was painful. But as I grew in faith and in the understanding of the ways of God, I allowed God's grace to penetrate my life more and more, and hear his voice, and I changed as a result. The change didn't happen instantly, though. And I know that there are still areas of my life where I've not surrendered to God's grace.

We must never forget though, that God can use us in our weakness. While I was staying at a retreat centre one time, an attractive girl invited me to her room for a chat. When I arrived, I discovered that she was only wearing her underwear. Because I'd invited God's grace into my life, nothing happened. And I ended up telling her the story of Our Lady of Guadalupe. The following morning, she said to me, *'John, last night I really felt a closeness to Our Lady for the first time in my life. And I understood her role in bringing us to Jesus.'*

God cares about each one of us and invites us to share in that freedom only he can provide. We are all his sons and daughters.

One time, I went to see Declan, an eighteen-year-old who I'd been helping through problems. His life was in a bit of a mess and he'd missed an important exam at school.

'My dad phoned up my physics teacher at school to find out when my exam was,' he said angrily when I walked in.

I suggested we went for a walk to help him cool down. *'Why do you think your dad rang up your physics teacher?'*

'To make me look an idiot.'

'No, he didn't do it to make you look an idiot. He didn't want you to miss

another exam. He cares about you.'

As soon as he realised this, his anger evaporated. When he saw his dad later that day the first thing he did was apologise.

God loves us even more than our parents are able to. And he's not complicated. If we ask him the question, he'll give us the answers.

****
****

Something to think about

And now, son, listen to me, never deviate from what I say.

Proverbs 5:7

Chapter 13

Gang Warfare

Looking back on my life as a gangster, I can now see the evil that was present in some of the situations I ended up in. I can remember times when I was gripped by sheer rage. If anyone crossed me, I released it. I became more and more brutal.

Evil and Satan are realities. There isn't any contradiction between a loving God and the existence of hell. We're all given free will by God. He wants us all to be saved but he doesn't force us to love him.

One time, Padre Pio gave a talk about heaven and hell and at the end a young man came up to him and declared he didn't believe in hell. Padre Pio looked at him and said, *'Don't worry, my friend, you will when you get there.'*

I don't believe there's much difference between the people in heaven and those in hell. They have both sinned. The difference is that the people in heaven admitted they had sinned and asked for forgiveness, whereas the people in hell said they needed no one apart from themselves. The key thing for all of us to do is to ask God for mercy.

Heaven is not guaranteed. At the moment of death each person will be judged on how they have lived their life. The Church calls this the 'particular judgement', as opposed to the 'last judgement' when all of humanity will be judged by God.

Jesus said, *'Do not be afraid of those who kill the body and after that can do no more. I will tell you whom to fear: fear him who, after he has killed, has the power to cast into hell.'*

God's mercy is wonderful, but we have to ask for it. God wants us to be in heaven a million times more than we could ever want to be in heaven. You have to accept the mercy of Christ. God sends no one to hell. People choose to go to hell. The Catholic Church teaches that hell is real, but it doesn't say anyone is there, because that would be judgement.

There's a cosmic battle for souls going on in the world between God and Satan. This was something that Tolkein showed in his trilogy The Lord of the Rings. God wants us in heaven more than we could ever know. But the Devil is trying his hardest to lead us not to heaven but to hell.

Witchcraft and Satanism aren't harmless, as some suggest. They're very dangerous. This is why every bishop is supposed to provide his diocese with an exorcist. My friend Jez told me about the time he went to see a teenager who was into death metal, a kind of satanic rock music. He and his friends had got some occult books from the library and started practising spells and curses. They saw that they had the power to make people have accidents. They also started desecrating churches. But one person they had no power over was Father Denis Herlihy, who prayed for protection against the Devil.

One night, the teenager was told by his mum that if he carried on dabbling with the occult he'd go to hell. This terrified him, so he went to see Father Hurlihy. Father Hurlihy prayed over him and asked for him to be delivered. He then asked Jez to go and see him. When Jez went to his room, he saw that there was a pentagram and other occult symbols on the walls. Not wanting to stay there, Jez took the teenager out for a coffee, and he talked to him about the dangers of the occult. Wisely, the teenager put an end to his occult practices. He's now a committed Catholic.

And I remember hearing the story of Betty Brennan. Because she felt lonely, even though she was married, she used to go to classical music concerts. She got chatting to the conductor one day and soon a friendship developed. He listened to her pour her heart out. Then one day he asked her if she wanted to go with him to a prayer group. She agreed, not knowing that it was a Satanic group.

Soon, she discovered that she had powers and she began to use them. One of her friends invited her to attend a Charismatic prayer group. When she went, she made the lights go out and the candles flicker. She was unable to stay at the consecration. On one occasion, she ran out of the church and straight into the arms of a priest, who knew instantly that she was in the grip of the Devil.

He prayed over her and she experienced the presence of God. She now travels around America, warning against getting involved in Satanism. She tells audiences that if you put a hundred altar breads on a table with only one of them consecrated, a Satanist would know which one that was.

A priest I know told me about the time he was woken up in the middle of the night by someone knocking at the door. Opening it, he found a smartly dressed stranger standing there.

'Father, I need you to pray over me,' said the man.

'What, now?' said the priest sleepily. *'Why?'*

'It's because I'm involved in a Satanic sect.'

Wondering if what the man was saying was true, he invited him in.

The priest listened as he told him about his life and how he had become involved in Satanism. *'My job in the sect is to go to motorway service stations between 1 a.m. and 4 a.m.'*

'Why?' asked the priest.

'I try to befriend people who look lonely and vulnerable.'

'But why do you do that?'

The man paused for a while and then said, *'I try and talk them into committing suicide.'*

One of the greatest examples of evil in recent times was the Nazi concentration camps, where an estimated six million men, women and children, most of them Jews, were murdered.

The camp commandant of Auschwitz was Rudolf Hoess. He was a happily married Catholic with five children. From his bedroom window, he could see the crematoria chimney stacks. He'd kiss his children goodnight after ordering the torture and gassing of countless Jews.

At the end of the war, Hoess was arrested and handed over to the Polish authorities. At his trial, he testified that Auschwitz had the capacity to exterminate ten thousand people in 24 hours, and he confessed to the killing of two and a half million people. He was sentenced to death, and returned to Auschwitz to be hanged on the gallows outside the entrance to the gas chamber.

Hoess seemed to see the way he disposed of all those human beings as a sort of gift he had. I couldn't understand how an intelligent, rational man could do this. What he did was pure evil.

I believe that a satanic wave can sometimes hit a country. This happened in Germany under Hitler and it happened in Rwanda when Tutsis and Hutus began slaughtering each other.

The Devil is very real and his aim is to destroy us as humans. One of the ways he tries to destroy mankind and create a void between God and us is to tempt us through sin. Hoess and those people in Rwanda acted in such an evil way because they were completely overtaken by the voice of evil. Sin is what the Devil uses to bring about havoc in the world. The more people ignore sin, the more Satan reigns.

I always mention sin in my talks. Sometimes, when I do an examination of conscience with kids in schools, I detect an awkwardness and that some think it's funny. Some sins, like lying, might seem small, but they have wider implications. I remember reading a poem that had the lines:

'Oh, what a wicked web we weave
When we first try to deceive.'

If you're being offered something that you know is stolen, you shouldn't take it. It will never bring you joy. I used to sell dodgy MOTs and insurance cover notes. When my brother-in-law heard about this, he said what I did was repugnant. When I asked him why, he said that by giving people a false MOT I was deceiving them into thinking the car was in good nick. *'What if the car isn't roadworthy and someone has an accident? You're responsible. And if someone with a fake insurance cover note hits a child crossing the road and he is seriously injured, his parents wouldn't get a penny to help with the medical bills.'*

Each one of us is a sinner, but each one of us is loved by God. I remember the time I attended a retreat led by Father John Edwards in Yorkshire. He came up to me one afternoon and asked if I'd pray with him over some people. I felt very privileged but also, as I told him, uneasy, as I was very sinful.

He said to me, *'All your sins are weaknesses.'* But it's important that we don't con ourselves about our sins. There's a spiritual war going on in our world between good and evil, even though we can't always see it. We should pray for the protection which God gives us.

Our world often dismisses the supernatural because it can't understand it. Many people try to explain away the miracles of the gospels. And books like The Da Vinci Code try to rationalise the supernatural.

When we feel that we are about to sin it's as if there are two voices in our head: one from the Devil saying *'go on, do it, you'll enjoy it'* and the one from Jesus saying, *'don't do this; it will hurt you.'* If we go ahead and choose sin, the voices change. The Devil then says, *'you are disgusting and horrible.'* But Jesus says to us, *'it's okay, I still love you.'* We are all prodigal sons or daughters.

Padre Pio said *'Fear is a greater evil than evil itself.'* Jesus came to liberate us from fear. During his ministry he accepted everyone and showed no fear. In those days, many people feared lepers. But Jesus embraced them.

We all need courage in our lives. Courage is not the absence of fear. It's the overcoming of fear. If we look at the lives of the apostles when they went out to proclaim the gospel, they had tremendous courage. We see it in the lives of St Joan of Arc, St Margaret Clitherow, St Thomas More and St Maximilian Kolbe. But this courage only came through the grace of Christ. We are all called to be courageous and to live for Christ.

Fear has nothing to do with God. It has to do with evil. If we know Christ and his strength, then we shouldn't be afraid. If we know we're loved, then we should have no fear. Mother Teresa was the most courageous person I've ever met. This was because she was so certain of God's love for her.

When I was a gangster, many people looked at me as being a hard man. But in truth I was a scared man. I was scared to such an extent that I wouldn't sit in a club unless I had my back to the wall, in case someone came in and shot me. As I've come to know Christ more and more, I'm not afraid of anything. The reason for this is because the most powerful person in the universe is my best friend. Know that the Devil's there; but don't give him too much credit.

Here are some tips to help you in your fight against the Devil:

Like a soldier gets armed for battle, we also need to put on our spiritual armour for the spiritual battle.

We need to live our lives according to Jesus' teachings and commandments.

When we sin we should immediately pick ourselves up and go to confession. A soul in a state of grace is aware of the Devil's tactics. Always trust that Jesus forgives us even the greatest of sins.

Attend Mass and receive Holy Communion as often as possible, even daily. Spend time in adoration of the Blessed Sacrament.

Set time aside in the day for personal prayer. Pray the rosary.

It's only in having a very honest and genuine relationship with Christ that his voice can be heard clearly.

Read scripture daily. Ignorance of scripture is ignorance of Christ.

Fast.

Use sacramentals, such as holy water, blessed salt, Miraculous Medals, crucifixes, scapulars etc.

Find a spiritual director.

Avoid occasions of sin – if you're on a diet, don't work in a doughnut factory.

Pray specifically for protection often, especially the St Michael and Guardian Angels prayers.

Don't be afraid of the Devil. As Saint Pio says, *'Fear is greater than evil itself.'*

Avoid the occult i.e. Ouija boards, tarot cards, fortune-telling, palm readings, astrology, witchcraft and New Age ideas.

Don't look for confrontation with evil. If it comes your way, don't try and handle it yourself.

The Devil's greatest tactic is to convince us he is not real.

His next tactic is to give people an unhealthy interest in him.

What are some of the signs that we could be under spiritual attack?

Discouragement, increased temptation to sin, disunity with those close to us, fear, anxiety and despair.

Be courageous with your faith. Share it with others. Stand up to the Devil, be strong in faith and he will flee from you.

Know your need of God. Don't kid yourself that you are stronger than you are.

Pride always leads to a fall.

Be obedient to the Catholic Church and to your spiritual director or priest.

Praise God. Always and everywhere thank God and constantly praise him for all situations – even if your house is falling down around your ears!

The joy of the Lord is our strength. The Devil hates joy.

Be careful what you watch, listen to or read. What we put into our mind has a massive effect on us.

Consecrate your life to Our Lady. She is the key to finding peace in Christ.

Pray for and with each other. None of us has all the answers on our own.

Know that you are loved and accepted unconditionally by God, and don't listen to the lies of the Devil.

Don't give in to scruples. Don't judge or criticise yourself. Allow God to be the judge. He is much more merciful than you are.

Invoke Our Lady and the saints. You are never alone.

Don't accept any negative thoughts. As Saint Pio said, *'Pray, hope and don't worry.'* The victory is already won.

Protection and Healing Prayer

Heavenly Father, I praise and thank you for all you have given me. Please cover me with the protective precious blood of your son Jesus Christ and increase your Holy Spirit in me with the gifts of wisdom, knowledge, understanding, hunger for prayer, guidance and discernment to help me know your will and surrender to it completely.

Father, please heal my negative emotions and any wounds in my heart. Send the sword of your Holy Spirit to sever and break all spells, curses, hexes, voodoo and all negative genetic, intergenerational and addictive material, past, present and to come, known or unknown, against me, my relationships, family, finances, possessions and ministry.

Father, I forgive and ask forgiveness for my sins and failings, and ask that my whole person, body, mind, heart, will, soul and spirit, memory and emotions, attitudes and values lie cleansed, renewed and protected by the most precious blood of your son Jesus.

In the name, power, blood and authority of Jesus Christ, I bind and break the power and effects in or around me of any and all evil spirits who are trying to harm me in any way and I command these spirits and their companion spirits in the name of the Father, the Son and Holy Spirit to leave me peacefully and quietly and go immediately and directly to the Eucharistic presence of Jesus Christ in the closest Catholic church tabernacle and be disposed of by Jesus and never again return to harm me.

Dear Holy Spirit, please fill up any void in me to overflowing with your great love. All this, Father, I pray in the name of Jesus Christ by the guidance of your Holy Spirit.

Immaculate Heart of Mary, Spouse of the Holy Spirit, please pray for and with me.

Amen.

****
****

Something to think about

Keep sober and alert, because your enemy the Devil is on the prowl like a roaring lion, looking for someone to devour.

I Peter 5: 8-9

Chapter 14

Giving Up The Gear

I've probably used every drug going. I did this because I was looking for a high. I didn't have a relationship with God then, so I placed false gods in my life. Apart from drugs, I also sought highs from sex and gambling.

I first got into drugs through smoking cigarettes. This then led to dope. Then I moved on to sulphate, which gives you a great high when you take it. But it doesn't last long, and when you come down you want to top yourself. I then moved on to Es.

I became involved in importing Es. The chemist who used to make them often put strychnine – rat poison – in them. For the people who bought them, it was a bit like picking up a gun with a bullet in one of the chambers and not knowing which one. Some people in the clubs died as a result of taking Es.

When Es no longer gave me the buzz, I started taking neat-washed crack cocaine, the most addictive drug in the world. At a talk in a prison once, I met a guy who was serving a mandatory fifteen-year sentence. This meant that he wouldn't be able to apply for parole but would have to serve all fifteen years. When I asked him what he was in for, he told me that he'd carried out seven armed robberies to pay for the ounce of crack he needed to take every day.

A friend of mine started smoking dope at fifteen. A year later, he was on heroin. He confessed that he bit lumps out of his arms because he hated the fact that he couldn't give up heroin.

Drugs will never fulfil you. They are the lies of the Devil and give us an illusion of what grace really is. Dope gives you a false feeling of peace. True peace only comes through God. The euphoria from cocaine leads to you becoming addicted to it. God offers you euphoria for free.

I meet a lot of kids who are addicted to porn on the internet. When I ask them how this happened, they usually tell me that it started by just looking at a site occasionally. It then became a driving force in their life. If you throw away the computer, then you lose all the good things it can be used for. It's better to bring God into your life and let him heal that addiction.

We're not culpable if we are truly

addicted to something. But it's our fault if we don't seek help. The person who has enabled me to be set free from my addictions is God. It's that higher power that Alcoholics Anonymous founder Bill W. talks about. We have to surrender ourselves and say, *'I can't do this on my own. I need your grace and strength to overcome this addiction.'* If we do this, God will always step in to help us.

I used to be addicted to gambling. One time, I only had a fiver to last me the week, so I asked God to increase it. I said to him that if he did this, I wouldn't gamble again. I went into a bookie's and won thirty quid. That was the last time I've ever gambled.

Many people struggle with addictions. Some people have addictive personalities. What we try to do with addictions is fill an emptiness in our hearts. We talk about addictions to gambling, drugs or drink, but there are many other things that we can become addicted to: sex, power, money, possessions, even people. I've a friend who is addicted to football. If Manchester United win, he's happy; if they lose, he's depressed.

But we shouldn't become depressed by our addictions. If we trust him, God can help us to change. Cardinal Newman once said, *'To live is to change, and to be perfect is to have changed often.'* There's no addiction that God cannot set us free from.

I remember speaking about sin to a guy who was a heroin addict. He'd overcome his addiction after living in a Cenacolo community for two years. But when he left, he returned to his addiction. When I asked him how this had happened, he replied, *'I put it down to swearing.'* His answer took me aback. *'Before I knew it all those boundaries I'd set when I lived in the community were broken. I started smoking dope, then I started going out with girls and going too far. All my morality went out the window. It was a slippery slope.'*

Many people start smoking weed and end up taking harder drugs. I saw this happen a lot in the East End. And I've seen it with some of the young people I've met. Drugs wreck lives. I've met many people whose lives fell apart through drugs. The mellow feeling that you get is illusory. It doesn't last. No drug can really bring you the peace and happiness you are searching for. I tried them all and, each time, I felt empty inside.

To break our addictions, as Bill W. says, you must surrender to a greater power. In other words, you have to know that you are helpless to overcome it on your own. You need something greater than yourself. We have to surrender our will and say to God that we can't do it on our own.

The Twelve Steps of Alcoholics Anonymous

1. We admitted we were powerless over alcohol – that our lives had become unmanageable.

2. We came to believe that a Power greater than ourselves could restore us to sanity.

3. We made a decision to turn our will and our lives over to the care of God as we understood Him.

4. We made a searching and fearless moral inventory of ourselves.

5. We admitted to God, to ourselves and to another human being the exact nature of our wrongs.

6. We were entirely ready to have God remove all these defects of character.

7. We humbly asked Him to remove our shortcomings.

8. We made a list of all persons we had harmed, and became willing to make amends to them all.

9. We made direct amends to such people wherever possible, except when to do so would injure them or others.

10. We continued to take personal inventory and when we were wrong promptly admitted it.

11. We sought through prayer and meditation to improve our conscious contact with God as we understood Him, praying only for knowledge of His will for us and the power to carry that out.

12. Having had a spiritual awakening as the result of these steps, we tried to carry this message to alcoholics and to practice these principles in all our affairs.

****
****

Something to think about

Look, I am going to send my
messenger in front of you
to prepare your way before you.

A voice of one that cries in the desert:
Prepare a way for the Lord,
make his paths straight.

Mark 1:3

Chapter 15

Get Real

I once lived with a girl called Charlie and her three-year-old son. But I shared very little about myself with her, or with anyone else in those days. I still felt the rejection I'd experienced as a child. I wasn't in touch with who I was. There was a lot of anger and bitterness in my heart. When our relationship broke up and Charlie moved out, she knew no more about me than when she'd moved in.

Finding out who we really are and who God wants us to be is crucial in the spiritual journey. One of my favourite stories is about a boy who is walking on a farm and he finds an egg, which he thinks is a chicken egg, because that's the only kind of egg he's ever seen. So he puts it in with the chickens. But really it's a golden eagle egg. The golden eagle hatches out and because he's surrounded by chickens he thinks he's a chicken and begins to peck around the farmyard all day long. One day when he's out walking with the other chickens, he looks up in the sky to see the most beautiful thing he has ever seen – a golden eagle.

'What's that?' he asks one of the chickens.

'That's a golden eagle,' comes the reply.

'I'd love to be a golden eagle,' he says.

'You're a chicken mate, so just get on with it,' says the chicken.

As the years go by, he carries on believing he's a chicken, because everyone tells him he is. But every now and again he thinks back to the most beautiful thing he's ever seen – the golden eagle. At last, he dies and goes to heaven, and Jesus says, *'My son, I so much wanted you to be the beautiful thing I created you to be.'*

Jesus loves us and he created us in his image and we're beautiful. It took me twenty-seven years to realise this. The chickens might be our friends, or our families, or the media, telling us we're no good and we need this product, this amount of money, to look like this model or to take this drug to be truly beautiful. It's a lie. The only thing we really need is God's love.

When Channel 4 broadcast a very derogatory programme about Mother Teresa, someone urged her to fight them. *'They're taking away your reputation.'* Mother Teresa replied, *'Well, that's one less thing to carry.'*

There was a thirteen-year-old boy who was very interested in aviation. But when his best friend was killed in a plane crash, he was so devastated that he locked himself in his room for three days and wouldn't come out. Naturally, his parents were getting very worried about him. On the third day he came out and handed his mum a Bible and said to her, *'I'm not afraid any more. I'm going to be a pilot.'* She was amazed that he had been reading the Bible, something he'd never done before. As she flicked through the pages she saw that he'd ringed three hundred and sixty-six times the words *'do not be afraid'*. That boy grew up to be Neil Armstrong, the first man to set foot on the moon.

In convents you often meet eighty-year-old nuns who look about fifty. This is because they have a beauty through Christ's presence in them. I once rang up Mother Gabriel and said, *'The closer I get to God the more I see my utter ugliness. I'm so lustful and so broken.''''But isn't it great?'* She replied, *'You've got it!'* St Paul never became down about his sinfulness because he'd been redeemed by Christ. He said it was the only thing he could boast about.

We all wear masks. We do this because we want to be loved. But when we go home and we shut our bedroom door, we don't have to pretend any more. There's no one to impress. We can be real. I believe that the more we stand up for what we know is right, the more people will respect us.

When I was a youth worker in Hackney, I found it very difficult to talk to Duane, a cocky teenager with a reputation as a tough guy. Every time I tried to talk to him he became aggressive and confrontational. One time, after I tried to sort out an argument with him and another kid over a pool game, he challenged me. *'Come on, then, what are you going to do?'* I could feel anger welling up inside me. I'd had enough of him and just wanted to hit him, but I kept my cool. When he eventually stormed off, part of me felt humiliated for backing down from a nineteen-year-old.

A short while later, while I was standing outside the youth club having a fag and trying to cool off, he walked past. When I asked him if he'd calmed down, he swore at me, but one of his mates urged him to talk to me, and to my amazement he trudged over to me.

'Listen! I don't like being touched,' he said with a stony stare.

I was stunned by this. Instead of a cocky, aggressive teenager who thought he was a hard man, I saw a broken kid who had shared something from deep within himself. He'd only said a few words, but I knew that what he'd said spoke volumes.

'It's all right. I understand,' I said. *'I was rejected when I was a kid. I'm sorry.'*

He studied me for a moment and then said, *'You're all right, man.'*

From that point on, I never had any problems with Duane. I understood something about where he was coming from. We often make rash judgements about people, not knowing what has shaped their life. I'd done that with him. As Gandhi said, *'you should walk for a mile in another man's shoes before you condemn him.'*

That barrier between us was only broken down because he was honest with me. Honesty is vital if we really want to let people know who we are.

When I was once talking to a priest about my relationship with my dad, he said, *'Allow your dad to be a dad.'* So I went to him and asked him for some advice. Now, I hadn't opened up with him about my life since I was a teenager. He was really touched, and he gave me some very good advice. I was allowing him to be a dad again. Our relationship began to blossom after that. Shortly before he died, he turned to me and said one day, *'I love you and I'm proud of you.'* I'd waited all my life to hear those words.

An important part of finding out who we really are is learning to be alone. And this isn't always easy. During my second spell in prison, when I was nineteen, I was placed in solitary confinement. I felt very angry and I was close to hating myself. I wanted distractions from myself. On the outside I had used sex and drugs as a distraction, but banged up in prison, I had to face me.

But it can be hard facing ourselves.

It sometimes seems easier to take on the identity of a group. When I lived in The Bronx there used to be a street gang called the 'Bloods'. Some of their members were as young as fourteen, and it contained girls as well as boys. To be accepted into the 'Bloods' you had to pass an initiation test. This involved riding the subway train with some other gang members and finding someone who was wearing red. It could be a child or an elderly person. You then had to slash them across the face with a knife. If you did this, you were in.

If you wanted to leave the gang, you had to ask permission. The gang members would take all the change out of their pockets and throw it on the floor. You then had to pick it all up before you left. While you were doing this, the other members would hit you with baseball bats. If you survived this beating, you'd be allowed to leave. In the eyes of the gang, you'd proved that you were hard enough and wouldn't grass them up if arrested by the police. You might think that no one would want to join a gang like this. But people are queuing up to – because they want to belong to something.

Discovering what our particular gifts are is part of discovering who we are. At school I used to think I was stupid. Later, I discovered I was very intelligent. The reason why I was made to feel backwards and stupid was because I had dyslexia.

I remember being at a talk from a woman who had spent time in a Nazi concentration camp. She said that when we die and go to heaven there will be a room full of chests. And in these chests will be all the gifts we've never used.

We shouldn't want the gifts others have, but be content with our own. Lots of the time we pray for extra gifts instead of grace to use the gifts we already have.

One of God's greatest gifts to us is our sexuality. Today though, sexuality is often seen as something we choose, not something given to us by God. We see men becoming more feminine and women becoming more masculine. Some men now use as many cosmetics as women. We hear more and more about transsexuals and transgender. One of the winners of the Channel 4 reality show Big Brother was a man who changed his sex to become a woman. This type of thinking undermines God's creation and his plan for us.

Our society sees beauty in physical terms. TV, magazines and pop videos are full of so-called beautiful people. Advertisers often tell us that if we buy this or that product, then it will make us beautiful. We also see how people can become false gods. Certain footballers, pop singers or other entertainers are almost worshipped. Many people look up to them, even though their lives away from the glossy images are a mess.

You can meet someone who is very pretty on the outside but dead as a doornail on the inside, because they don't know God's love. Mother Teresa on the other hand, looked a bit like a shrivelled up prune, yet she was one of the most beautiful people you could ever meet. She was completely transparent to God's love.

When the fashion industry encourages women to wear sexually provocative clothes, it's saying the only way you can be loved and adored is to wear short skirts or low cut tops. Working on the doors, I saw that many girls used sex to get love and many of the guys used love to get sex.

A girl who used to live with me in the community told me about when she used to dance semi-naked in cages in a nightclub. At the end of the evening all the guys would hit on her, thinking she was easy. She said she found it one of the most demeaning experiences of her life.

Our parents give a lot to us, but sometimes we don't see it. Many teenagers tell me that their parents force them to go to mass on Sundays. I always reply that the only reason their parents do this is because they love them and care about them. It's like the story of the girl who was playing in the street. Her mum shouted to her that she wanted her back home in five minutes. The girl complained to her friend and said that she wished her mum was like her mum, who let her stay out until all hours. But the other girl replied, *'I wish my mum was like your mum; I wish she cared about me.'*

Sometimes people ask me why I spend all my time giving talks in schools, parishes and prisons. They seem to think that I'm not free. It's hard work, but I'm more free and fulfilled now than I've ever been in my life. In the old days when I would take drugs, sleep around and do generally what I wanted, I wasn't fulfilled.

Mother Teresa wisely remarked that if you tell people the truth, they have a choice about whether to accept it or not. The truth's not to be found in the messages of advertisers or in wealth and fame, or in sexual fulfilment with another person. None of these will fulfil you. The truth is to be found in Christ, who invites each one of us to allow him into our life and makes us the person God wants us to be. Only then do we start to become truly free.

****
****

Something to think about

If you make my word your home,
you will indeed be my disciples:
you will come to know the truth,
and the truth will set you free.

John 8:32

Chapter 16

Poseurs

The way I got into organised crime was by doing backstage security at concerts by Queen, Bruce Springsteen, Status Quo and other rock stars. These stars were treated like gods by their fans, some of whom would go to amazing lengths to get near them, to get an autograph or to touch them.

But when we look at these idols, we have to ask: what sort of values do they present to us? I remember a magazine voting as 'Man of the Year' a rock star who was taking crack and heroin and was an active homosexual. This was saying, *'It's okay to take drugs and okay to be promiscuous.'* The Krays, who terrorised London's East End, have achieved cult status. Yet people who knew the Krays told me that they often behaved like animals.

Father Stan Fortuna, a New York friar who performs rap music, says we should always be aware of the words of a song and ask ourselves about the lifestyle of the artist. If a singer is sleeping around or taking drugs, it's unlikely that their music will be uplifting. Music goes into our soul. If the music is angry it can make us angry. Good Christian music, such as Delirious, Rich Mullins or WOW Worship can be very uplifting and help you to become more aware of God.

Real heroes are those men and women who overcame their difficulties to live for Christ and others. In some cases they even gave their life. Pope John Paul II lived through Nazi occupation in Poland and went on to become one of the greatest spiritual leaders of the Church. He refused to compromise the truth. As he travelled the world, he spoke out against evil, stood up for the unborn and the poor, and played a key role in bringing down Communism. He called men and women to turn back to God, where their true happiness would be found. He wasn't bothered that his message was unpopular with some people.

The millions of people who flocked to Rome when he died in 2005 showed what an effect his life had had on the world. Even many who disagreed with his teaching held him in great respect because he stayed true to his beliefs.

The person I chose for my confirmation Saint was St Thomas More.

To me, he was someone who was an outstanding human being. He refused to sign an Act, which would make King Henry VIII the head of the Church in England. He believed that the Church was built on St Peter and that no monarch could replace this. At his trial, he said, *'This is a repugnant law which no one can make. No one can say they are the head of Christ's Church on earth.'* Christ said St Peter was the head of the Church on earth. His authority was passed to the popes that followed him. Before St Thomas More died, he said, *'I die the king's good servant; but God's first.'* He stands out as a man of extraordinary bravery and faith. He served God, not the world. A true celebrity.

In the world we live in today the media likes to tell us how we need to look like this film star, pop star or model to be beautiful. It's a world where men and women pay thousands of pounds to have their appearances altered through cosmetic surgery. As a result of this obsession with the perfect body, a lot of us feel we are ugly and that we're not worth much.

Many people look to their body to find the ultimate fulfilment in life. The reason suntan lounges and fitness centres are often full of mirrors is because they are about vanity. When we look at Pope John Paul during the last months of his life, we can see someone who was truly beautiful because of his heart shining through. In the world's eyes though, he was just a geriatric. But he was loved and adored because he loved and he gave.

We don't need the world to tell us that we are beautiful. All we have to know is that God loves us, then we'll know that we're beautiful. Advertisers tell us that without their brand we are worthless. If we're not wearing Nike trainers or don't have the latest Sony phone, then our name means nothing. It's their name that matters. We don't need someone else's name to make us who we are.

We're told that the more money we have, the happier we will be. When I was earning thousands of pounds a week from drug deals, inside I felt empty. Money doesn't satisfy. We can see this from the number of wealthy people and celebrities who end up in rehab clinics or commit suicide.

Affluence and success can be a danger in the spiritual life. It's noticeable that as Ireland has become more materialistic, with its large houses and bungalows springing up everywhere and its 24-hour Tescos in many towns, some people seem to be turning their back on God. When Ireland was poorer, people were more dependant on God. A priest once remarked to me, "The sooner the Celtic tiger is shot, the sooner people will return to God."

In Christianity we now have what is known as the prosperity gospel. This means that God rewards you materially. The preachers who promote this message often fly in personal jets and drive flashy cars. St Francis of Assisi spoke of the freedom to be found in poverty. When I came to Ireland I only had fifty quid in my pocket. I now live in a nice house with the community. But if God said to me in the morning, 'leave it all', I would.

I'm not against wealth. Money can do a lot of good in the world. I've met many wealthy people who give generously to good causes. Many of them do it without any publicity. St Paul didn't say that money was the root of all evil. He said that love of money was the root of all evil. The important thing is not to become attached to it.

Pope John Paul lived out his faith through suffering. St Thomas More gave his life rather than reject the Church. It's people like these, not pop stars and other celebrities, who we should try to emulate. They know the real meaning of fulfilment, because they've put God at the centre of their lives.

****
****

Something to think about

So if anyone declares himself for me in the presence of human beings, I will declare myself for him in the presence of my Father in heaven. But the one who disowns me in the presence of human beings, I will disown in the presence of my Father in heaven.

Matthew 10: 32-33

Chapter 17

It's Sorted

During the fifteen years I've spent with God, I've discovered that the more I've got to know him, the more peace I've felt in my heart and in my life. Many times I look back and I wonder why was it that I experienced more peace in one situation than another. When I reflect, I see it was at times when I really trusted God. Trusting in God is an important part of our faith journey.

An example of how I learned to trust in God was when I was living rent free in a presbytery in North London. I was also drawing the dole and getting money from my flat, which I'd rented out. I started to feel that this wasn't right. In prayer one day, I felt Our Lady say to me that the truth would set me free. So the next morning, I signed off. Later that day, I received a cheque from a friend for £400.

That was eight years ago. Since then, I haven't signed on. I've lived entirely off God's providence. He's fed me, clothed me and I haven't gone without a bed.

This reminds me of a story I heard about a man who slipped while he was walking up a mountain. Reaching out, he managed to grab hold of a tree.

Terrified, he called out, *'Is anyone there?'*

'Yes, I'm here,' said God.

'Save me!' screamed the man.

'I'll save you,' said God. *'Let go of the branch.' 'Is there anyone else there?'* shouted the man.

Many times in our lives God asks us to let go. One time, I had a dream in which I was driving a car and fighting with the steering wheel because the car wouldn't go where I wanted it to go. But when I let go of the steering wheel the car went exactly where I wanted it to go. The point of this dream was that I needed to let go and let God drive my life. When I was a gangster, I tried to drive my own life, and I made a complete mess of it. In the last fifteen years I've tried to let God drive it.

But we have to use our common sense when we trust God. We can't just sit there and wait. There was once a woman caught up in a flood, so she prayed to God to help her. A dinghy arrived at her house and a man urged her to get in.

'No, I'm waiting for God to save me,' she replied.

As the water became higher, she went up into the attic. A sailing boat then came along and a man shouted to her to get in.

'No, I'm waiting for God to save me,' she called back.

As the waters rose even higher, she climbed up onto the roof. Then a helicopter appeared and the pilot dropped a winch for her. *'Grab hold of it,'* called the pilot.

'No, I'm waiting for God to save me,' replied the woman, who was now standing on the chimney pot.

The waters then swept her away and she was drowned. She arrived in heaven to be met by Jesus.

'Jesus, you said you would take care of me. Why didn't you?' demanded the woman.

'What do you mean?' replied Jesus. *'I sent a dinghy, a sailing boat and a helicopter.'*

Trusting God is not complicated. He will direct us if we trust in him. If I look at the last fifteen years of my life, the time I have been with God, I can honestly say that I haven't walked anywhere where God wasn't leading me. Those fifteen years seem almost like a jigsaw. Everything fits together.

Spiritual direction is very important in trusting God and in our Christian journey. A spiritual director acts as a guide. It might be your parish priest or someone recommended to you. Usually you meet with a spiritual director once a month and talk through the ups and downs of your spiritual journey. Through spiritual direction, I've been helped to really grow in my faith.

When I was working as a volunteer in the East End, I had no money to buy food or pay the bills. I was always borrowing money until I got my giro cheque. I said to Jesus, *'You told me that when I followed you I'd receive everything I needed. If it's your will that I don't have any money to buy food until my giro comes on Thursday, then I accept it. But if it's not could you give me some money.'* A few minutes later, a friend of mine turned up at my flat and asked me if I'd help him to tow his car. Afterwards, he gave me twenty quid. That was enough money to get me through to Thursday. To me, that was a sign of God's providence.

I remember hearing a talk at World Youth Day in Paris by the late Cardinal O'Connor of New York. He told of how he was flying as a co-pilot in a bomber during the Second World War when he discovered that they were running out of fuel. The other pilot was more concerned that he would get into trouble for not taking on board enough fuel than that the plane might crash.

The pilot decided that they would have to make an emergency landing, but the thick fog made it very difficult. One of the engines then developed problems. Cardinal O'Connor felt sure that they were going to be killed. All of a sudden a voice from the control tower could be heard: *'I'm going to lead you in. Trust me and listen to me.'* The plane landed safely.

This story illustrates how we must trust God. God never stops loving us. Whatever we need, he'll give us. Like that man clinging to the tree on the mountainside, we just have to let go.

****

Something to think about

So do not worry about tomorrow: tomorrow will take care of itself.

Matthew 6: 34

Chapter 18

Kiss Of Death

I often speak about abortion when I visit schools and I sometimes use a story of a fifteen-year-old girl I know to illustrate the horrendous damage that abortion can cause.

When she discovered she was pregnant she felt unable to tell her father, so she left home and went to stay with her older sister. Eventually, she plucked up the courage and phoned her father to tell him. He was angry and threatened to kill her if she came back home.

Her sister arranged for her to have an abortion and the girl was admitted to a clinic. The doctor injected a salt solution into her womb to bring about a premature birth. This should have happened almost immediately but, for some reason, it took hours. When the baby was born the girl took it in her hand. It was a boy. Looking at him, she felt that she wanted to place him back in her womb so that he might live again.

Afterwards, she went to stay with one of her other sisters, who had two beautiful children. But she couldn't bear to touch them because of the emotional pain she felt at having aborted her own child. She began to feel hatred against her sister who had arranged the abortion, her father and, most of all, herself. A series of abusive relationships with different guys then followed. She felt this was all she deserved.

One day, she was walking in the park, feeling very low, when a stranger walked up to her and gave her a prayer card. On the front was an image of Our Lady of Czestochowa, who had scars on her face. The girl took one look at the picture and began to cry. She felt that Mary carried scars on her face because, like her, she knew what it was to lose an innocent son.

After this, the girl invited God into her life and sought his mercy. She's now happily married with three children. She works full-time with the pro-life movement in America, trying to persuade other women not to make the same mistake as her, or if they have, showing them God's mercy.

A baby is one of the most beautiful gifts that God gives us. And each baby is sacred because it is created in the image and likeness of God. Someone once said that each newborn baby is a sign that God has not forgotten us. Jesus came to us as a helpless baby, totally dependant upon the love, care and protection of Mary.

Today though, every year hundreds of thousands of women in the West choose to have abortions, believing that they have a right to decide what to do with their body. Our bodies though, belong to God, and are temples of the Holy Spirit.

We live in what Pope John Paul II called a 'culture of death', where abortion is often presented by some as just another form of contraception. You get people who make a fuss about saving trees or foxes but say nothing about abortion. The Government spent hours of time in the House of Commons debating fox-hunting and then banned it. Why don't they do this with abortion? Our society has a bizarre idea of morality.

Those who campaign for abortion deny that what a woman is carrying in her womb is a living human being. This is nonsense. What else could it be? I once saw a sticker on a car that said, *'Abortion – one dead, one wounded.'*

In 1994 Mother Teresa was invited by President Bill Clinton to join political and religious leaders for the National Prayer Breakfast in Washington D.C. Previous speakers had avoided controversy. However, Mother Teresa didn't.

She spoke passionately about the rights of the poor and the unborn. She said abortion was the greatest destroyer of love and peace. What gave Mother Teresa's words such power was that she backs them up with action. Her children's home in Calcutta had saved over three thousand children from abortion. She once remarked, *'To say there are too many children is like saying there are too many flowers.'*

Brother Martin told me about a woman who attended one of his weekends for women who have had an abortion. The idea is to help them experience the forgiveness of God. When this woman came away from confession she was in floods of tears.

'Are you okay?' asked Brother Martin.

'When I was nineteen I had an abortion. I tried to put it out of my mind and out of my life. But a year later I found myself getting quite depressed. So I started drinking a lot with my friends. By the age of twenty-one I was clinically depressed and an alcoholic. I lived with both of these crosses for thirty years. Recently, my counsellor was changed and his replacement was a Catholic. He went back into my life and the abortion came up. He suggested I came on this weekend. I heard about God's love and mercy, so I went to confession. There's two things I now know after that confession. I met God's mercy and I realised that God loves me. Why didn't someone tell me this thirty years ago? If they had, I wouldn't have lived with all this pain.'

I was once taking part in a prayer vigil outside an abortion clinic in The Bronx. As the doctors passed by I said, *'Jesus loves you. And he loves the babies you're killing. Please stop killing these babies.'*

Some time later, several of the doctors came up to me and one of them said, *'You have to pray for us for the rest of your life because we've just made a pact that we aren't going to carry out another abortion as long as we live.'*

Afterwards, Father Andrew said to me, *'You always have to do this in love, John. I love those doctors. Because of this, God used my love to convert them.'*

A friend of mine who had an abortion decided to have her baby named Teresa and baptised. This gave her a great sense of peace. Many years later, she was in Rome, and she found herself thinking about the baby. She prayed that she might meet her baby in heaven. One day, she was standing next to a fountain. Suddenly she noticed that inscribed on the stone were the words, *'I love you, Mummy. Teresa.'* She saw this as a sign that her baby was waiting for her in heaven.

We should cherish life from the moment of conception to natural death. There are those who want to legalise euthanasia. They say there is no reason for a person's suffering. Christ on the cross revealed that there is a reason for suffering. This reason is redemption. St Paul said that the crucifixion wasn't over and that he wanted to be a part of it and offer up his suffering for Christ and for the redemption of the world. We can do that also.

When my dad was dying in hospital,

he said that he saw a reason for his suffering. *'I can unite myself with Christ.'* Euthanasia is a grave evil because it destroys this opportunity to unite ourselves with the suffering of Christ.

There was once a man looking in the window of a jeweller's shop when he noticed an amazing pearl. He was fascinated by it and decided he must have it. When he entered the shop Jesus was standing behind the counter. The man asked Jesus if he could have a look at the pearl. Jesus showed it to him.

'Can I touch it?' asked the man.

'Yes,' said Jesus.

Holding it in his hand, he felt that he had everything he'd ever wanted in his life. When he handed it back to Jesus, the feeling immediately left him.

'How much does it cost?' he asked.

'It's very expensive,' replied Jesus. *'How much money do you have?'*

'I've got £50,' replied the man.

'Okay, give me that,' said Jesus.

So he did. Then he said, *'But how will I get home? That's the only money I have.'*

'Oh, so you have a home. Give me your home,' said Jesus.

'But what about my wife?' 'So you have a wife. Give me your wife,' said Jesus.

'If I do that, there's no one to look after my children,' said the man.

'Oh, so you have children. Give me your children.'

'If I do that,' said the man, *'what's the point of me working. I will only have a dog.'*

'Oh, you have a dog,' said Jesus. *'Give me your dog.'*

Jesus asked the man for everything he had. He gave him everything he owned. Jesus gave the man the pearl. Even though the man felt fulfilled at receiving the pearl, there was a sadness in his heart because he was leaving so much behind.

As he was about to walk out the door, Jesus called him back.

'Here's your £50,' he said. *'But remember it doesn't belong to you. I'm*

only loaning it to you. Here's your wife back, but remember she's mine. She doesn't belong to you. Here's your children back, your home, your dogs. But remember, they belong to me.'

Life is a tremendous gift from God. We're called to cherish it, not cheapen it. We must never lose sight of the fact that each person is created in the image of God.

****
****

Something to think about

You created my inmost self,
knit me together in my mother's
womb.
For so many marvels I thank you;
a wonder am I, and all your works are
wonders.

You knew me through and through,
my being held no secrets from you,
when I was being formed in secret,
textured in the depths of the earth.

Your eyes could see my embryo.
In your book all my days were
inscribed,
every one that was fixed is there.

Psalm 139: 13 – 15

Chapter 19

Pearly Gates

As human beings nothing ever completely satisfies us. We might think it will, but when we get it, it doesn't. I found this out through the drugs I took and all the wads of money I earned. Ultimately, I ended up feeling empty and thinking there had to be more to life. Jesus rose from the dead to offer us the chance of a new life in heaven.

I believe that heaven will be total fulfilment and euphoria. In heaven we will be completely and utterly satisfied in every way, and we'll overflow with joy. This is what I live for.

A man once described to me how he felt when he held his newborn baby son in his arms for the first time. Grinning, he said that he felt a joy he couldn't express. This kind of joy must be a reflection of what heaven is like. But I believe that it still doesn't come close to describing it.

Yet many people try and create heaven on earth. 'Money, money, money', sang the pop group Abba. We live in a world where we're told that the more money we have, the happier we will be. We feel that if we have more money, we'll be happier. But we won't. It's in giving that we receive, not taking. Even though we may be poor we can be rich in spirit.

In the book *The Final Quest* by Rick Joiner, one of the characters is shown heaven and then returns to earth. He sees all these people at the bottom of the mountain who are being shot to pieces by demons. He asks Jesus why they're standing there being shot when they could climb the mountain. *'They're stupid,'* he says.

Jesus answers, *'They're not stupid. These are the evangelists and the prophets. They're more concerned about getting others to the top of the mountain than getting themselves there. And these are the angels who are begging God to minister to them. These are the most important people in heaven. They are willing to sacrifice their own lives for others.'*

St Augustine, one of the great thinkers of the Church, said, *'Our hearts are restless, Lord, until they find rest in you.'* He was someone who had searched for God in all the wrong places before undergoing a conversion. He'd even fathered a child out of marriage.

A priest who was dying was asked, *'What will you do when you get to heaven?'* He replied, *'Well, if I get to heaven, I will ask God if I can spend my first thousand years of eternity just looking at the Milky Way.'* He'd always been awestruck by the stars and planets he saw when he gazed into the sky at night.

In heaven we'll experience a joy beyond our wildest dreams. Nothing we experience now will compare with it. St Paul says of heaven, *'What no eye has seen and no ear has heard, what the mind of man cannot visualise; all that God has prepared for us.'* We should never try to create heaven on earth, but be prepared to give everything up that gets in the way of heaven. It's worth selling everything we possess and giving God everything for it. I like the story of the rich woman who turns up at the gates of heaven.

'You're very rich, aren't you?' said St Peter.

'Yes,' she replied.

'Well, you're lucky. You've just got in. Follow me. I'll show you where You'll live.'

He then takes her to a street of beautiful mansions.

'This is great,' she enthused.

But he then takes her to a field with a hut made of corrugated iron standing in it. *'This is where you'll live,'* he tells her.

'You must be joking,' she said indignantly. *'I lived in much better places than those mansions when I was on earth.'*

'Well, I'm sorry', replied St Peter, *'but this is the best we could do with what you sent up.'*

The more we do for God on earth, the more treasure we will store up in heaven. No matter what we may have done, or not done, God wants each of us to be with him in heaven.

One day, a man arrived at the gates of heaven and was met by St Peter, who told him he needed ten points to get in. He then asked him what he'd done with his life.

'I was a good Catholic,' said the man.

'That's one point,' said St Peter.

'I had my children baptised and brought them up as good Catholics.'

'That's two points,' said St Peter.

'I was a good husband and always tried to be honest.'

'That's three points,' said St Peter. *'Anything else?'*

But the man couldn't think of anything else.

'I'm sorry,' said St Peter, *'you didn't get the ten points.'*

Just as he is closing the gates, the man asked, *'What if I throw myself at the mercy of God?'*

'Well,' said St Peter, *'that's ten points straight away. Come in.'*

I remember when my friend Neil and I were relaxing on the beach in Haifa in Israel. It was one of those amazing sunny days with a clear blue sky when you just feel the joy of God. On our way back to our hotel, Neil turned to me and said, *'I felt God the Father say, "If you think this is good, wait until you get to heaven."'*

On another occasion, in the church in Downside Abbey, I was completely overwhelmed by the presence of God in the Blessed Sacrament. I felt there was nowhere else in the world where I wanted to be. I could have stayed there for all eternity. When I came out of the church I thought to myself, if God can fulfil me so much in all my weakness, sin and pain now, how much more can he fulfil me when I reach heaven?

Eternity is a very long time, so let's use our time wisely now, so that we reach it. I remember a young guy who decided to become a Catholic. For a year, he attended an RCIA (Rite of Christian Initiation of Adults) course each week. Eventually, he was baptised, made his first confession and was confirmed. The next day, he was killed in a car accident. At the time, he didn't know that this year was preparation to meet Jesus.

I believe that we should work towards our heavenly home and not try to make ourselves rich in this life. When I was a gangster, I used to have everything that the world says will make you happy – loads of money, a penthouse flat, flashy cars, women – and I was completely empty. Now I have very little, but I work for that treasure which cannot decay: being with God in heaven.

Someone once remarked to me that when we die we're going to find ourselves walking through a tunnel into the biggest football stadium we've ever seen. And there on the terraces will be all the angels and saints. When someone like Mother Teresa enters that stadium, the cheers that go up will shake the world we live in. When Jesus was hungry, she fed him. When he was naked, she clothed him. When he was in prison, she visited him. And when he was thirsty, she gave him a drink.

When we walk through that tunnel, what sort of response will we get for what we've done with our life? I pray that we get a greater cheer than even Mother Teresa got and that we receive that pearl of great price, our heavenly Father. The words I live for are, *'Come in good and faithful servant.'*

****
****

Something to think about

One of the rulers put this question to him. 'Good Master, what shall I do to inherit eternal life?' Jesus said to him, 'Why do you call me good? No one is good but God alone. You know the commandments: You shall not commit adultery; You shall not kill; You shall not steal; You shall not give false witness; Honour your father and your mother.' He replied, 'I have kept all these since my earliest days.' And when Jesus heard this he said, 'There is still one thing you lack. Sell everything you own and distribute the money to the poor, and you will have treasure in heaven: then come follow me.' But when he heard this he was overcome with sadness for he was very rich.

Luke 18: 18–23

Chapter 20

Inside Information

Here's what I like to call some inside information for those who want to meet God in their lives:

Always be yourself in front of God and others. Never pray to impress anyone. Never act in a way to impress others.

Never be led by fear. Fear is nothing to do with God. When you sin always get up and go to confession.

The journey to God has to start from the heart, not the head.

To be beautiful, the only thing we need is to know we are loved by God.

God loves you just as much the millionth time you confess a sin as the first time you confessed it.

If we were perfect, then we wouldn't need redemption and forgiveness.

It's in our weaknesses that God uses us.

Change doesn't happen overnight

Sin doesn't hurt God as much as refusing to love your brother as yourself.

God is present in each person we meet.

God never asks us to be successful, but to be faithful.

Don't compare yourself to others. You don't have to be the best – just do your best.

Prayer is the oxygen of the spiritual life.

It's not the amount of time you spend in prayer that matters, but how real you are when you pray.

When we pray, it should be because we love God, not because we have to pray.

Pray the rosary.

We'll never be perfect until we meet God in heaven.

God loves you in your sexuality. We must accept all of ourselves, especially our sexual tendencies (but this doesn't mean that we act on them). Only God can get in and heal any brokenness.

If you're on a diet, don't work in a doughnut factory. If you are tempted to access porn sites on the internet, don't have your computer in your bedroom. Put it in the living room, where all the family goes. The same applies to TV.

If you are struggling with remaining chaste with your girlfriend, don't spend time alone with her in your bedroom. Spend time together in more public settings.

All spiritual growth depends on honesty with yourself and God.

Find someone with whom you can be honest and real. This might be a priest, spiritual director, friend or someone in your family.

Make small sacrifices each day – if you really want that cream cake, don't have it.

To be real for Jesus we need his body and blood. Go to mass and adoration.

Don't judge yourself. Allow God to be the judge – he's much more merciful than you.

If you're ever in doubt about how much God can change you, just look back over your life.

We don't make ourselves holy. Only God can do this.

Read about the lives of the saints.

Put some holy pictures or statues in your bedroom. These are like photographs and remind us of loved ones in heaven. A small shrine in your house is another good idea.

Wear blessed objects, such as a crucifix, scapular or Miraculous Medal.

Mary helps us to see our true selves, without condemning ourselves when we look through her eyes.

God trusted Mary with our salvation, so how much more can we trust her with everything.

God made you the way you are for a reason. Never doubt it.

If you would like to meet Jesus, then join me in saying this prayer:

Serenity Prayer

Lord Jesus, I give you my life and I give you everything I am.

I ask you to use me in my weakness and in my strength, so that I may always glorify you.

I am sorry for all the sins I have committed.

Help me always to confess my sins to you when I fall down and help me always to remember that you love me and have set me free.

Lord, I give my life to you and I ask you to use me to help others. Help me to become a great saint, Lord and to bring many faithful souls to you.

Help me to know that it's through giving that we receive; through giving tirelessly even until it hurts.

Help me to know that all happiness comes through service of you. Let me die to self, Lord, and live for you.

Let me know that through being completely in touch with your love I can glimpse heaven on earth, for heaven is being in touch with your love, truth and grace.

I give my heart, mind, body and soul to you to do with me as you will.

Not my will but your will be done.

I choose you to be my Lord and my saviour from this day forward.

Amen.

Glossary

Blessed Sacrament – The consecrated bread in which Jesus is present. See *Tabernacle*.

Communion – Jesus Christ received under the forms of bread and wine during Mass. See *Eucharist*.

Confession – A Sacrament where a person confesses their sins to a priest who grants forgiveness in the name of Jesus. It is also known as penance or reconciliation.

Divine Mercy Prayer – A prayer given by God to Sister Faustina, a Polish nun, in 1935, and now recited by many Catholics.

Eucharist – The Eucharist was instituted by Jesus at the Last Supper and is the main act of worship for Catholics. The term is used for both the service – more commonly called the Mass – and the bread and wine, which the priest consecrates.

Friar – A member of a religious community, such as the Franciscans or Dominicans.

Gospel – The good news of Jesus. There are four gospels: Matthew, Mark, Luke and John.

Evil – The opposite of good; anything which goes against the will of God.

Grace – the Help God offers us to live in accordance with his will and discover fulfilment and happiness.

Heaven – the place or state where those who have attained salvation enjoy eternal happiness with God.

Hell – The place or state inhabited by Satan and the fallen angels.

Holy Spirit – The third person of the Trinity.

Mass – See *Eucharist*.

Medjugorje – A place of pilgrimage in Bosnia-Herzegovina where the Virgin Mary is said to have appeared to a group of young people.

Miraculous Medal – A medal bearing the image of the Virgin Mary received by St Catherine Laboure during a vision in the nineteenth century.

Nun – A female member of a religious community, often called a religious sister.

Pope – The successor of St Peter who has received the authority to govern the Catholic Church in the name of Christ.

Prayer – The raising of the mind and heart to God. It can be vocal or silent.

Purgatory – The place or state of cleansing before entry into heaven.

Reconciliation – See *Confession.*

Retreat – A period of time usually devoted to silence, prayer and reflection.

Rosary – A popular form of prayer in which scenes from the life of Jesus are meditated upon through using rosary beads.

Sacraments – Visible signs of invisible grace. There are seven sacraments: baptism, Eucharist, confirmation, reconciliation, marriage, holy orders, and anointing of the sick.

Saint – A person of outstanding holiness now with God in heaven.

Satan – A being – also called the devil – opposed to God and seeks to destroy goodness.

Sin – An action which breaks divine law. Sin entered the world through the disobedience of Adam.

Spiritual director – A person, often a priest or nun, who offers guidance in growing spiritually.

Tabernacle – A special box in which the Blessed Sacrament is reserved in churches.

Trinity – The doctrine that states God is one but made up of three persons, Father, Son and Holy Spirit.

Virgin Mary – The mother of Jesus, who remained a virgin throughout her life.

Also available

For more information go to
www.johnpridmore.com

To the Holy City
1670-2020